3

TIME ZONES

WORKBOOK | THIRD EDITION

DAVID BOHLKE
ANDREW BOON

NATIONAL
GEOGRAPHIC
LEARNING

Australia · Brazil · Mexico · Singapore · United Kingdom · United States

NATIONAL GEOGRAPHIC LEARNING

National Geographic Learning,
a Cengage Company

Time Zones Workbook 3 Third Edition
David Bohlke and Andrew Boon

Publisher: Andrew Robinson

Managing Editor: Derek Mackrell

Associate Development Editor: Don Clyde Bhasy

Additional Editorial Support: Sarah Jane Lewis

Director of Global Marketing: Ian Martin

Senior Product Marketing Manager: Anders Bylund

Heads of Regional Marketing:
   Charlotte Ellis (Europe, Middle East and Africa)
   Kiel Hamm (Asia)
   Irina Pereyra (Latin America)

Senior Production Controller: Tan Jin Hock

Associate Media Researcher: Jeffrey Millies

Senior Designer: Lisa Trager

Operations Support: Rebecca G. Barbush,
   Hayley Chwazik-Gee

Manufacturing Planner: Mary Beth Hennebury

Composition: Symmetry Creative Production, Inc.

For permission to use material from this text or product,
submit all requests online at **cengage.com/permissions**
Further permissions questions can be emailed to
permissionrequest@cengage.com

ISBN-13: 978-0-357-42639-5

National Geographic Learning
200 Pier 4 Boulevard
Boston, MA 02210
USA

Locate your local office at **international.cengage.com/region**

Visit National Geographic Learning online at **ELTNGL.com**
Visit our corporate website at **www.cengage.com**

Printed in the United States of America
Print Number: 01 Print Year: 2020

CONTENTS

1

I'D LIKE TO BE A **PILOT**

PREVIEW

A Match. Join the two parts of the sentences.

1 An accountant ○   ○ **a** treats sick or injured animals.

2 A doctor ○   ○ **b** performs songs.

3 A pilot ○   ○ **c** keeps financial records.

4 A singer ○   ○ **d** flies an airplane.

5 A vet ○   ○ **e** treats sick or injured people.

B Read the job descriptions. Match them with the jobs from **A**.

1 a job that involves working with pets _____

2 a job that involves a lot of math _____

3 a job that allows you to improve people's health _____

4 a job that allows you to be creative _____

5 a job that involves a lot of traveling _____

C Write. List four more jobs which allow you to be creative.

_____

_____

LANGUAGE FOCUS

A Complete the sentences. Circle the correct answers.

1 He'd like a job that involves **to work / working** with children.

2 She wants to **be / work** a flight attendant.

3 What does he **like / want** to be someday?

4 I'd like a job that allows me **traveling / to travel**.

5 She wouldn't **like / likes** a job that's dangerous.

6 What **do / would** you like to do someday?

7 I **want / would** a job that involves **to work / working** in a team.

8 Ryan has a part-time job which allows him **studying / to study** at college too.

B Complete the sentences. Use the correct form of the words and phrases in the box.

creative	dangerous	travel
research work	work with students	work outside

1 Zoe wants to be a tour guide. She wants a job that allows her _____ .

2 Tim plans to study art in college. He'd like a job that's _____ .

3 Ross would like to work in education. He'd like a job that involves _____ .

4 Asha doesn't want to be a soldier. She doesn't want a job that's _____ .

5 Caitlyn wants to be a scientist. She wants a job that involves _____ .

6 Kai doesn't want an office job. He wants jobs that allows him to _____ .

C Complete the conversation. Number the sentences in the correct order.

a __1__ Hi! Please come in. How can I help you?

b _____ OK. Let me see. What kind of job would you like?

c _____ Yes, I do. I don't want to work in the evenings or on weekends.

d _____ OK. Finally, is there anything else you want to add?

e _____ Hello, Mr. Burns. I'd like some advice on what to do after I finish school.

f _____ And do you want a job with regular hours?

g _____ Yes, there is. It has to pay well, too!

h _____ I'd like a job that involves working with numbers.

THE WORLD'S BEST JOBS

80% of firefighters are happy with their jobs.

A Read the article. Circle the correct answers.

What are some of the best jobs in the world? According to some sources, the happiest workers are firefighters, writers, teachers, artists, and nurses. Firefighters are happy because their job allows them to help people in trouble. Writers and artists often do not make much money. However, they enjoy their work because their jobs are very creative.

Some teachers find their jobs difficult and leave within five years. Those who stay, however, say they enjoy having a job that allows them to work with people—teachers like helping students and watching them grow. Finally, even though they often work long hours, nurses have a high amount of job satisfaction. They find happiness at work by helping others.

1 The best jobs include creative jobs and jobs that _____ .

   a allow you to help people   **b** pay a lot of money   **c** are challenging

2 According to the article, writers and artists _____ .

   a make a lot of money   **b** do creative work   **c** help people

3 Some _____ quit within five years because they find the job difficult.

   a firefighters   **b** nurses   **c** teachers

B Answer. According to the article, which jobs allow you to help people?

_____

_____

READING

A Skim the article. Choose a different title.

a   The Dangerous Job of a Shark Tank Cleaner

b   The Important Job of a Shark Tank Cleaner

c   The Creative Job of a Shark Tank Cleaner

WORKING WITH SHARKS

A job as a cleaner may not sound very fun or exciting. But what if it involves putting on a wetsuit and diving into a huge tank full of sharks every day? As a shark tank cleaner at the New York Aquarium, this is what Mark Adams does.

5   The job of a shark tank cleaner is an important one. Cleaning the tank every day helps keep the sharks healthy and happy. Mark and his team pick up any food that the sharks do not eat—if food is left in the tank, it will go bad. The divers also clean off the algae (small green plants) that grow on the glass. If the cleaners do not clean the glass, visitors won't be able to see inside the tank.

Mark loves his work. Sometimes, as he cleans the tank, he even waves to visitors.
10   Swimming in a tank full of sharks may sound like dangerous work, but the sharks are used to people, and Mark feels safe when he dives. "We go through a long training program," Mark explains. "I'm confident and I enjoy my job." Of course, the sharks are well fed. "When we get in the tank, they're not that hungry!"

Nonetheless, shark tank cleaners never dive alone. Mark always goes into the tank with
15   another diver while another team member watches from the top of the tank. The three communicate using radios and hand signals. Mark says, "Sometimes we stop cleaning when the sharks have too much energy. But we've had no serious problems, and really want to keep it that way."

B   Answer the questions about *Working with Sharks*.

1   DETAIL   The shark tank at the New York Aquarium is _____.

   a   big   b   small   c   medium-sized

2   INFERENCE   The sharks eat _____ of the food that the workers give them.

   a   all   b   most   c   a small amount

3   DETAIL   The most important reason to clean the tank is to _____.

   a   allow divers to greet visitors

   b   keep the sharks healthy

   c   let visitors see the sharks

4   DETAIL   Which of the following do tank cleaners NOT do?

   a   undergo training   b   dive alone   c   wear a wetsuit

5 INFERENCE When do the sharks get fed?

    a before Mark gets in the tank

    b while Mark is in the tank

    c after Mark gets out of the tank

C   EXAM PRACTICE   **Read the sentences.** Circle **T** for True, **F** for False, or **NG** for Not Given.

1 Mark cleans the tank once a week.	**T**	**F**	**NG**
2 The sharks often get sick.	**T**	**F**	**NG**
3 Mark has to clean the side of the tank.	**T**	**F**	**NG**
4 Mark thinks his job is very dangerous.	**T**	**F**	**NG**
5 Mark sometimes stops when cleaning the tank.	**T**	**F**	**NG**

VOCABULARY

A **Complete the paragraph.** Use the words in the box.

> equipment   potential   proud   remote   researchers   train

Astronauts are good at many things. They know how to use all kinds of ¹ _____,
and they are prepared for almost any ² _____ problem. Astronauts prepare for
space travel by going to the most ³ _____ parts of Earth. They go there to
⁴ _____ in tough conditions, to help prepare them for space. It's a dangerous
job, but astronauts are ⁵ _____ of what they do. They hope that the work they
do in space will allow scientists and ⁶ _____ on Earth to learn new and
amazing things.

B **Complete the sentences.** Use the -*ous* form of the words in the box.

> adventure   danger   fame   nerve   outrage   poison

1 Cleaning a shark tank is not very _____ because the sharks are well fed.

2 Neil Armstrong is _____ for being the first person to walk on the moon.

3 Some parts of the blowfish are _____, so you can't eat them.

4 My cousin is a very _____ eater. She loves to try new things.

5 I'm sometimes _____ before exams.

6 The prices in that new restaurant are _____!

WRITING

WRITING TIP SUPPORTING YOUR OPINION: GIVING REASONS

One way to support your opinion is by giving reasons. Use phrases such as **the first reason,
one reason,** and **another reason** to introduce reasons.

A Read the model passage. Notice the phrases for introducing reasons.

I think Koharu should be a tour guide. There are three reasons why I believe this.

The **first reason** is that she is very outgoing and talkative. She is always talking with her friends, and she likes meeting new people. **Another reason** is that she wants a job that allows her to use her language skills. A tour guide needs to be able to speak different languages to visitors. The **final reason** is that she knows a lot about history. She often gives me information about the buildings in our city and helps me with my history homework.

For these reasons, I believe Koharu would be an excellent tour guide.

> State your opinion in the topic sentence.

> Give reasons in supporting sentences.

> Summarize your opinion in the concluding sentence.

B Think about a job you'd like to have in the future. Why would you like to have this job? Make notes.

C Write a paragraph. Use your notes from **B**. Include reasons and a concluding sentence.

_____

_____

_____

_____

_____

_____

_____

_____

_____

_____

2

WHICH ONE IS BRUNO?

PREVIEW

A **Complete the sentences.** Circle the correct answers.

1 Akira never gets angry about anything. He's very **interesting / easygoing**.

2 I always have a good time with Michael. He's **shy / fun to be around**.

3 I like talking to Ricardo. He always has something **outgoing / interesting** to say.

4 Alice never says very much. She's **kind of quiet / outgoing**.

5 Wendy makes me laugh so much. She's really **funny / interesting**.

B **Complete the sentences.** Use the correct form of the phrases in the box.

> sit in the front   wear sunglasses   hold a backpack   look at her laptop

1 Mei is the one who _____. I think she's checking her email.

2 Kevin is the one who _____. He never takes them off.

3 Liz and Jen are the ones who _____. They go everywhere together.

4 Julia is the one who _____. It's full of sports equipment.

C **Write.** What is your best friend like? Describe him or her.

_____

LANGUAGE FOCUS

A Match. Join the questions and the answers.

1 What's your sister like? ○   ○ **a** They're the ones watching TV.

2 Which one is Sheila? ○   ○ **b** She's the one sitting alone.

3 What does she like? ○   ○ **c** She's shy, but she's really nice.

4 Which ones are her parents? ○   ○ **d** They're pretty easygoing.

5 What are her parents like? ○   ○ **e** She likes music and art.

B Rewrite the sentences. Correct one mistake in each sentence or question.

1 What's Mei likes?

_____

2 They're the ones who is watching baseball.

_____

3 Steven is one checking his phone.

_____

4 John and Sue are the one who are having a party.

_____

5 Celia's the one who standing by the door.

_____

6 Which one are your cousins?

_____

C Complete the conversation. Use the phrases in the box.

> extremely outgoing   really helpful   pretty funny   kind of quiet

Adam: Yuki, did you make any new friends during your first week of school?

Yuki: Yeah, I did! There's Li Ping. She's [1] _____. She explains everything to me when I don't understand. I'm already good friends with her and Tammy Millar.

Adam: That's great. What's Tammy like?

Yuki: She's very nice, but she's [2] _____. I think she's a little shy. Oh, by the way, do you know Luka?

Adam: Is he the one who's always joking and saying crazy things?

Yuki: That's him. He's [3] _____. He always makes me laugh.

Adam: Yeah. And he's [4] _____, too. He's always at parties, and he's friends with everyone!

A SCHOOL IN THE MOUNTAINS

A local guide carries heavy climbing gear down the Khumbu Icefall.

A Skim the article. The Khumbu Climbing School wants to teach its students that climbing is:

1 _____

2 _____

Nepal's Khumbu Climbing School teaches locals how to be good climbing guides. They learn how to use climbing equipment, give first aid, and climb ice walls. They also learn how to communicate in English. The school encourages its students to see climbing as both a serious job and something to enjoy. After students finish the course, they can work as guides for the many tourists who come to the Himalaya to climb. In fact, many of the guides in the Himalaya are graduates of the school.

Max Lowe's parents were the ones who started the school in 2003, and Max knows the school well. He visits Nepal often and works hard to help out. In 2013, when the school celebrated its 10-year anniversary, Max visited and made a short video. He interviewed the instructors and showed how they train their students. Max hopes to continue his work with the school in the future.

B Read the article. Circle **T** for True or **F** for False.

1	The Khumbu Climbing School teaches tourists to climb.	**T**	**F**
2	Many Himalayan guides graduated from the Khumbu Climbing School.	**T**	**F**
3	Max started the school in 2003.	**T**	**F**
4	Max made a video about the school 10 years after it opened.	**T**	**F**

READING

A **Skim the article.** Underline all the things Sherpas do to help climbers.

PROTECTORS OF THE HIMALAYA

A The Sherpa people are the unsung heroes of mountaineering in the Himalaya. They are known for their excellent climbing skills, and they are famous for being strong, friendly, and dependable.

B There are around 150,000 Sherpas in Nepal, and many live in the most mountainous parts of the country. For them, mountain climbing is a part of everyday life. This is what makes them excellent guides. Many Sherpas use their climbing skills to help other climbers from around the world carry food, equipment, and bags up the mountains. They also choose the best climbing routes, set up camps, and cook meals as they guide people to the top.

C Before the 20th century, life was very different for the Sherpas. They were mainly farmers who raised animals. But as more people came to the Himalaya each year to climb, the Sherpa way of life changed. For many, mountain climbing became a main source of income. Being a climbing guide is a job that pays Sherpas well. But it's also very dangerous. Many accidents happen, and about 40 percent of the climbers who die each year are Sherpas. In 2014, for example, 16 Nepalese climbers died in the same accident. Thirteen were Sherpas. It was a terrible day for the Sherpa people.

D But the Sherpas continue to see the Himalaya as a place of spiritual importance. They also see themselves as protectors of the mountains. They work hard to protect the plants and animals there, and to keep the mountain environment clean. In return, the Himalaya gives the Sherpa people food, work, and a home.

E It's an age-old partnership—one that shows no signs of going away.

B **Answer the questions about *Protectors of the Himalaya*.**

1 `DETAIL` What is NOT true about the Sherpas?

   a They're known for their strength.

   b They help people climb mountains.

   c There are 1.5 million Sherpas in the country

2 `INFERENCE` Which of these words best describes Sherpas?

   a hardworking   **b** shy   **c** impatient

3 `DETAIL` Before the 20th century, the Sherpa people were mainly _____.

   a climbing guides   **b** farmers   **c** cooks

4 DETAIL   One downside of working as a climbing guide is that it _____ .

   a is dangerous   **b** harms the environment   **c** pays poorly

5 VOCABULARY   An *age-old partnership* (paragraph E) is one that _____ .

   a helps the elderly   **b** has existed a long time   **c** will last forever

C EXAM PRACTICE   **Match.** Join each paragraph to its main topic.

1 Paragraph A ○   ○ **a** how mountain climbing changed Sherpas' lives
2 Paragraph B ○   ○ **b** the relationship Sherpas have with the mountains
3 Paragraph C ○   ○ **c** why Sherpas are excellent guides
4 Paragraph D ○   ○ **d** what Sherpas are known for

VOCABULARY

A **Complete the paragraph.** Use the words in the box.

achieved   attached   completely   designed   giant   transformed

Phurba Tashi [1] _____ a rope to the climber and helped him up the mountain.
The climber was [2] _____ exhausted, but Phurba managed to get him to the
top and back down safely.

When mountain climbing became popular in Nepal, it [3] _____ the lives
of many people. Phurba is one such person. He started out as a cook, but today, he's a
[4] _____ in the mountain-climbing community. He holds the record for most
climbs up mountains higher than 8,000 meters. But an earthquake in 2015 changed
everything. It killed many people and destroyed the hotel Phurba [5] _____
and built. Phurba retired from climbing, but he still organizes climbs for others. Because
of Phurba, many have [6] _____ their climbing dreams.

B **Complete the sentences.** Use the words in the box. Use a hyphen when necessary.

last minute   much needed   well written   well known

1 After a difficult four-day climb, they took a _____ break.
2 Don't wait until the _____. Start now, while you still have time.
3 Phurba Tashi is _____. He's famous around the world.
4 That's a really _____ article. It explains the problem so clearly.

WRITING

WRITING TIP SUPPORTING YOUR OPINION: GIVING EXAMPLES

In Unit 1, you learned how to support your opinion by giving reasons. Another way to support your opinion is by giving examples. Use phrases like the ones below to introduce examples.

A **Read the model paragraph.** Notice the phrases for introducing examples.

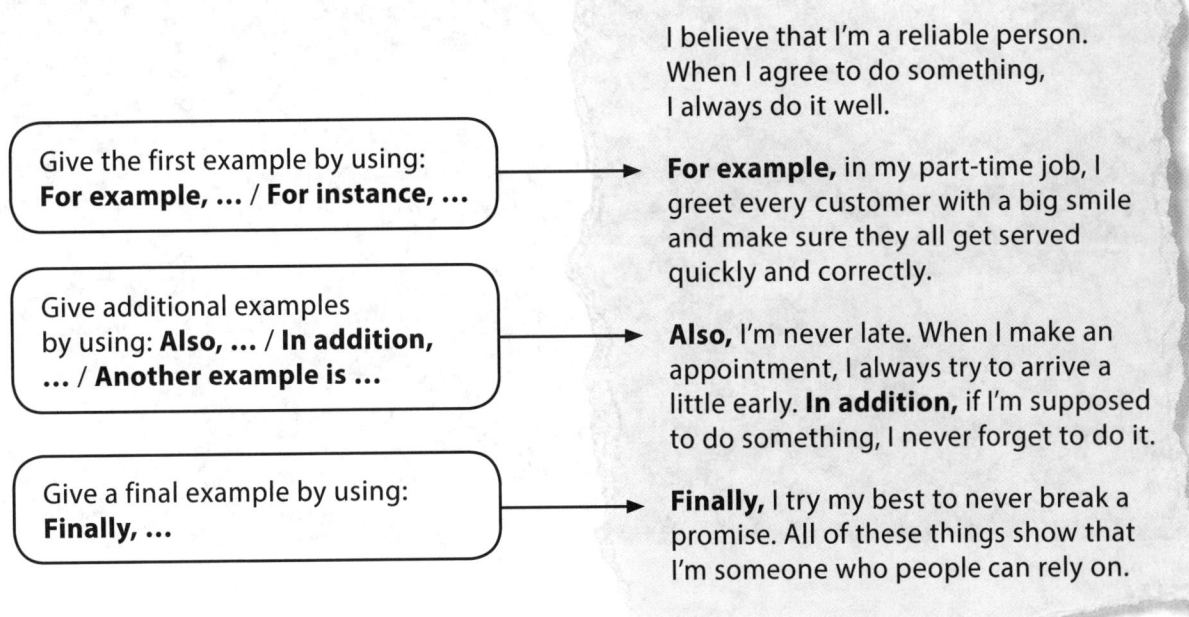

Give the first example by using:
For example, … / For instance, …

Give additional examples by using: **Also, … / In addition, … / Another example is …**

Give a final example by using:
Finally, …

I believe that I'm a reliable person. When I agree to do something, I always do it well.

For example, in my part-time job, I greet every customer with a big smile and make sure they all get served quickly and correctly.

Also, I'm never late. When I make an appointment, I always try to arrive a little early. **In addition,** if I'm supposed to do something, I never forget to do it.

Finally, I try my best to never break a promise. All of these things show that I'm someone who people can rely on.

B **Think of a word that describes your personality well.** List everyday examples to show how this word describes you. Make notes.

C **Write a paragraph.** Use your notes from **B**. Include examples and a concluding sentence.

_____

_____

_____

_____

_____

_____

_____

_____

_____

_____

_____

_____

3

WE HAVE TO REDUCE **TRASH!**

PREVIEW

A Cross out the word that does not belong.

1 reusable **bags** / ~~trash~~ / **cups**

2 **air** / **reusable** / **ocean** pollution

3 single-use **pollution** / **plastic** / **straws**

4 biodegradable **material** / **plastic** / **law**

B Complete the sentences. Use the words in the box.

> less   more   recycle   reduce   reuse

1 People need to use _____ plastic.

2 We need to _____ the amount of trash on our beaches.

3 We should use _____ biodegradable materials instead of plastic.

4 When you _____ , you need to separate plastic from paper.

5 Don't throw that bag away. You can _____ it the next time you go shopping.

C What is the worst kind of pollution where you live? What can we do to fix it?

_____

_____

LANGUAGE FOCUS

A **Unscramble the words to form sentences and questions.**

1 here / aren't / you / stand / to / allowed

_____ .

2 wear / a uniform / she / at / to / has / her new school

_____ .

3 to / we / in / class / allowed / our phones / are / use

_____ ?

4 you / take / food / the computer room / can't / into

_____ .

5 we / tickets / have / buy / to / today / do

_____ ?

6 can / both / this recycling bin / put / and plastic / into / paper / we

_____ .

7 the park / allowed / am / in / my bike / why / not / to ride / I

_____ ?

B **Rewrite the sentences and questions.** Use the words in parentheses.

1 I need to buy a reusable straw. (have) _____ .

2 We're allowed to leave early today. (can) _____ .

3 Do we need to bring our own bag? (have) _____ ?

4 Can I put my things here? (allow) _____ ?

5 You're not allowed to park there. (can't) _____ .

6 Are we allowed to bring our own food? (can) _____ ?

7 He can't play his music loud. (allow) _____ .

C **Match.** Join the parts of the conversation.

1 Hey, Ling. How's your recycling poster coming along? ○   ○ **a** Well, I want to put it in the school cafeteria, but I can't.

2 Where are you going to put it? ○   ○ **b** Yes. I'm allowed to put it in the hallway.

3 Why not? That's the perfect place for it. ○   ○ **c** Thanks! See you around.

4 That's too bad. Did she tell you where you can put it? ○   ○ **d** The principal said there are already too many posters there.

5 That's good. Well, I have to go. I can't wait to see it! ○   ○ **e** It's going great. I just have to find a few more photos.

THE REAL WORLD

ECO-FRIENDLY TRAVEL

The Parkroyal hotel in Singapore has "sky gardens" to lower its carbon footprint.

A Skim the blogpost. Choose another title for it.

a Reducing Food Waste   b Carbon-Friendly Tours   c Choosing a Green Hotel

Traveling is great fun, but it can also hurt the environment. So how can we stay green while traveling? Try staying at an eco-friendly hotel!

The first thing to do is to look for a carbon-neutral hotel. These are hotels that try to use less energy. They also use a lot of recycled materials and sell locally grown food. Some ban cars, and a few allow guests to buy carbon credits—guests pay a tax for any extra carbon they use. This money is used for clean energy or tree-planting projects.

Next, check the hotel's menu. Many hotels offer locally grown, organic food, and some even grow their own food in their gardens. Also, find out what the hotel does with the food that no one eats. In the United States, people and businesses throw away about 40 percent of the food they buy. Ask hotels what they do with food that's left over or that goes bad.

Finally, find out if the hotel uses a lot of plastic. Stay away from hotels that don't have rules against using single-use plastic items like straws, plastic bags, shampoo bottles, and water bottles, and look for ones that try to use as few of these plastic items as possible.

B Read the blog post. Complete the sentences. For each blank, use one word.

1 In some carbon-_____ hotels, _____ are not allowed.

2 A carbon _____ is a _____ you pay for the extra carbon you use.

3 Try staying at hotels with _____ grown _____ food.

4 Find out what hotels do with _____ that's left over or that goes _____ .

5 Stay at hotels that have _____ against using _____ plastic items like straws.

READING

A **Skim the article.** Label the paragraphs with these headings.

a Show That Every Bit Counts　　**b** Paint a Picture　　**c** Work with Others　　**d** Teach Them How

BE THE CHANGE!

Do you recycle, but find that people around you don't?
Most people know that recycling is important, but many
don't do it. For those who do their part regularly, this
can be disappointing. However, if you're someone who
5 recycles, don't worry—there's good news! There
are things you can do to encourage the people you
know to get on board with recycling:

Separating materials for recycling

1 _____
Use real-world examples to explain to people how
10 much of a difference recycling makes. Find photos of
places with too much trash and stories of places that
got better through recycling.

2 _____
Explain that every single item we recycle helps make a difference. For example, did you know
15 that recycling just one soda can saves enough energy to run a TV for three whole hours?

3 _____
Show people how to separate materials for recycling. Help them see that it's easy, and
that it doesn't take much time. You could also create a simple "how to" guide to help
them remember.

20 **4 _____**
Start a neighborhood recycling club. Meet up with other people who recycle, and think
of ways to make recycling easier where you live. Or make recycling fun by organizing a
neighborhood cleanup or a recycling art contest.

Changing people's minds isn't easy, but it's not impossible either. Just be honest about
25 why recycling is important to you, and you'll be surprised by the number of people who listen and
make small changes in their lives.

B **Answer the questions about *Be the Change!***

1　PURPOSE　The article is for people who _____ to recycle.

　　a don't want　　　　　　**b** don't know how　　　　　**c** want others

2　VOCABULARY　What does *get on board with* mean in line 7?

　　a learn about　　　　　　**b** participate in　　　　　　**c** tell others about

3　DETAIL　Which tip might involve you giving someone a prize?

　　a tip 2　　　　　　　　　**b** tip 3　　　　　　　　　　**c** tip 4

4 DETAIL According to the article, which of these is difficult to do?

   a separating materials   **b** making a difference   **c** changing people's minds

5 INFERENCE Which statement would the author probably agree with most?

   a Most people won't recycle unless you push them hard.   **b** Even small changes in people's recycling habits are helpful.   **c** We have to follow all four tips before we can get others to recycle.

C EXAM PRACTICE **Look at the diagram.** Complete the sentences.

1 Americans recycle about a third of their

   _____ .

2 Americans recycled about the same percentage

   of paper as _____ .

3 Americans recycled _____ the least.

US recycling rates, 2019

VOCABULARY

A **Complete the sentences.** Use the words in the box.

| annually   avoid   ban   reveal   solution   tax |

1 We need to find a(n) _____ to the plastic problem.

2 Some cities completely _____ cars in the downtown area on weekends.

3 The surveys _____ that more people are using reusable shopping bags.

4 I try to _____ buying items with a lot of plastic packaging.

5 How much food do you think we waste _____ ?

6 People should pay a small _____ when they buy plastic cups.

B **Complete the sentences.** Use the words in the box. Add *re-*, *-able*, or both. You can use some words more than once.

| fill   notice   new   use |

1 There was a hole in his shirt, but it wasn't very _____ .

2 My library book is expiring, so I'm going to _____ it.

3 He raised his hand and asked the waiter to _____ his glass.

4 She always comes up with interesting ways to _____ old items.

5 To fight climate change, we need to use more _____ energy.

6 You should keep that wooden straw. It's _____ .

WRITING

WRITING TIP **DESCRIBING WHEN THINGS HAPPEN**

When writing, you can use time words and phrases to help describe when things happen.
Here are some examples:

Before
When, While
As soon as, After

A **Read the model paragraph.** Notice the time words and phrases.

My school has many rules. **As soon as** we get to school, we have to go straight to our classrooms. If we're late, we have to apologize and ask our teacher for permission to enter **before** we can go inside and sit down. We aren't allowed to use cell phones **while** we're in class, but we can use them **when** we have breaks. For lunch, we can either bring our own meals or eat the cafeteria food. But we have to stay on school grounds. **After** the school bell rings at the end of the day, we're allowed to stay in school to study or do sports. But we have to leave school **before** five.

B **Think about the rules you have to follow at home.** What are some things you have to do and some things you aren't allowed to do? Make notes.

C **Write a paragraph.** Use your notes from **B**. Include time words and phrases.

_____

_____

_____

_____

_____

_____

_____

_____

_____

_____

_____

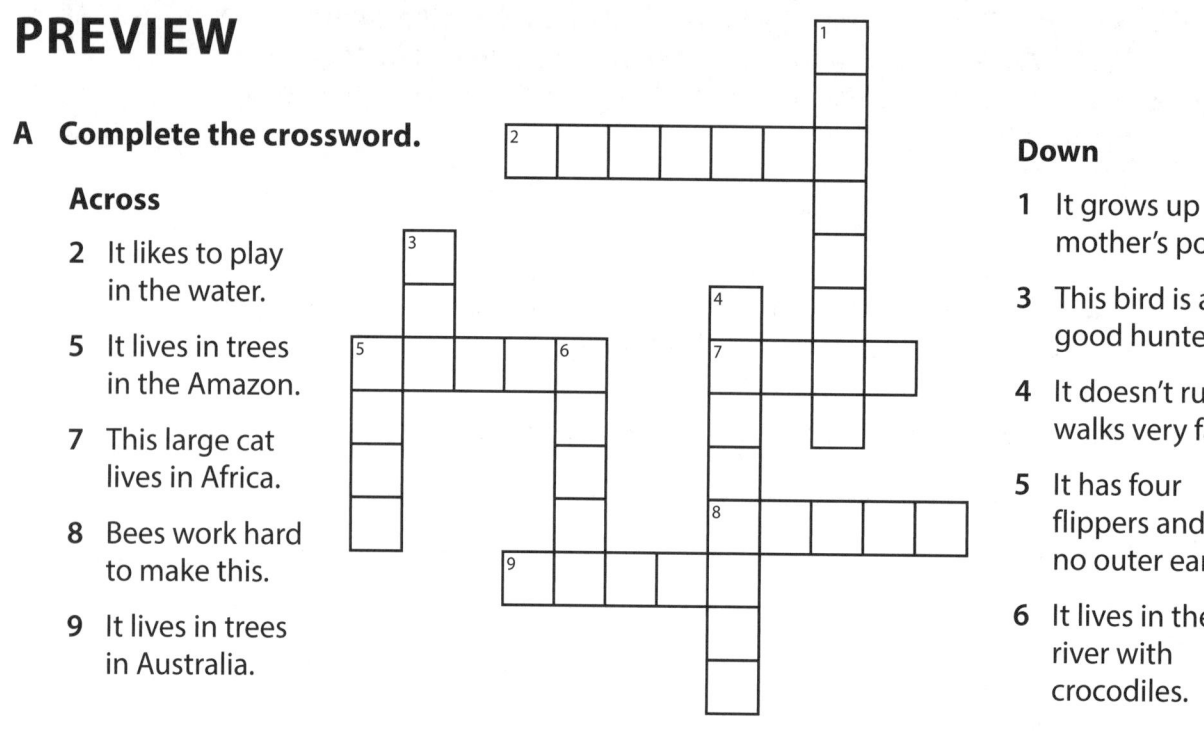

4

HOW DO SLOTHS MOVE?

PREVIEW

A Complete the crossword.

Across

2 It likes to play in the water.

5 It lives in trees in the Amazon.

7 This large cat lives in Africa.

8 Bees work hard to make this.

9 It lives in trees in Australia.

Down

1 It grows up in its mother's pouch.

3 This bird is a good hunter.

4 It doesn't run. It walks very fast.

5 It has four flippers and no outer ears.

6 It lives in the river with crocodiles.

B Complete the sentences. Circle the correct answers.

1 Sloths move **slowly** / **softly** in trees.

2 Owls hunt very **loudly** / **patiently**.

3 Dolphins swim **gracefully** / **sleepily** in the water.

4 Bats fly **badly** / **quickly** through the air.

5 Cats run **patiently** / **playfully** around the house.

C Write two sentences about yourself. How do you run, move, swim, or sing?

_____

LANGUAGE FOCUS

A **Complete the paragraph.** Circle the correct answers.

The bald eagle is the symbol of the United States. This [1] **powerful / powerfully** and [2] **beautiful / beautifully** bird has [3] **good / well** eyesight that it uses to spot fish up to 1.5 kilometers away. When it sees a fish under the water, it flies down [4] **quick / quickly** and [5] **expert / expertly** grabs its prey. Bald eagles are also very [6] **good / well** at building nests. They usually make their nests at the top of tall trees.

B **Rewrite the sentences.** Use adverbs.

1 Rabbits are fast runners. ___Rabbits run fast___.

2 Dogs are noisy eaters. _____.

3 Robins are beautiful singers. _____.

4 Bees are hard workers. _____.

5 Tigers are patient hunters. _____.

6 Elephants are good swimmers. _____.

7 Bats are quiet but quick flyers. _____.

8 Kangaroos are ferocious fighters. _____.

C **Complete the conversation.** Number the sentences in the correct order.

_____ Really? How fast can they run?

_____ I'm sure he understands more than you think! Oh, it says here that elephants smell really well. They can smell water up to 18 kilometers away.

__1__ Hey, Lisa. What are you reading?

_____ Up to 130 kilometers an hour. But they can only run fast for short periods of time. Here's another interesting fact. Some dogs can easily understand up to 250 words.

_____ That's a great idea! Let's have pizza.

_____ Oh, just an article about animals. Listen to this. Did you know that cheetahs are the fastest land animals on earth?

_____ Hmm. I don't think my dog understands that many words.

_____ Speaking of smell, I smell food. Let's have lunch!

THE REAL WORLD

THE LIVES OF FUR SEALS

A fur seal swims in the ocean.

A **Skim the article.** What threat did fur seals face in the past? What threats do they face today?

Past: _____   Today: _____

A Fur seals are named for the thick fur that covers their bodies. However, there are actually many different types of fur seals. Northern fur seals live in Canada and parts of Asia. The South American fur seal lives as far south as Antarctica. And several other fur seal species live in warmer waters near the United States, Mexico, Africa, and Australia.

B Fur seals come in different sizes. Some are over 3 meters long and weigh over 300 kilograms! They see and hear very well, which makes them good hunters. They are most comfortable in the water. They swim quickly and gracefully, sometimes spending weeks at sea eating fish, squid, birds, and tiny creatures called krill.

C Fur seals are beautiful animals, but their soft fur makes them attractive to hunters. In the 19th century, humans killed many fur seals and almost wiped the species out. Fortunately, in 1911, several countries banned fur seal hunting, and their numbers grew. Today, fur seals face other challenges, like overfishing and pollution.

B **Read the article.** Circle the main purpose of each paragraph.

1 Paragraph A _____.

   a shows that fur seals have to travel great distances

   b describes different kinds of fur seals around the world

2 Paragraph B _____.

   a describes how fur seals look and behave

   b explains why fur seals are so happy in the water

3 Paragraph C _____.

   a describes how hunters killed fur seals

   b explains the different threats fur seals face

READING

A Scan the article. Find and circle five adverbs.

FINDING NEW ANIMALS

Do you know how many kinds of plants and animals there are in the world? Experts believe there are between 8 and 14 million, but right now we only know about 1.5 million. However, scientists
5 are finding new plant and animal species all the time—and that's good news for us.

The smallest frog in the world.

In 2009, a university professor named Christopher Austin and his student Eric Rittmeyer discovered a new animal species. They were in Papua New Guinea, studying the wildlife on the island. One evening, they were in the jungle listening to animal sounds. The most
10 common sound was the noise of frogs croaking loudly. But there was another sound—a much softer, high-pitched one that sounded like it came from something much smaller.

At first, they couldn't locate the sound, but after some time, they realized it came from the ground. They searched through the grass and dead leaves carefully, but what they found surprised them. It was a tiny frog—just seven millimeters long. "This frog has a call that
15 doesn't sound like a frog at all," said Austin. The frog they discovered was the smallest in the world!

Researchers believe that frogs are important because they help keep the environment clean. We can also use them to create new medicines. Whenever we find a new species, we learn new things. For that reason, scientists work very hard to find new plants and animals
20 every day. But their jobs are getting tougher. The forests that these animals live in are disappearing quickly. And, sadly, so are the animals.

B Answer the questions about _Finding New Animals_.

1 `DETAIL` How many kinds of plants and animals haven't been found yet?

   a less than 1,000,000   **b** about 1,500,000   **c** more than 6,000,000

2 `DETAIL` Why were Austin and Rittmeyer surprised when they found the frog?

   a There weren't any known frogs in the area.

   b The frog's color matched the leaves perfectly.

   c It didn't seem like the sound came from a frog.

3 `INFERENCE` Austin and Rittmeyer probably expected to find _____ in the grass.

   a an insect   **b** an owl   **c** a rabbit

4 `PURPOSE` The purpose of the last paragraph is to show that _____.

   a finding new species is important

   b frogs are useful animals

   c scientists can use animals to make medicines

5 DETAIL The author says that researchers' jobs are getting more difficult because there are fewer _____ .

    a researchers   **b** labs   **c** animals

C EXAM PRACTICE **What does the article say?** Match the two parts of the sentences.

1 Austin and Rittmeyer ◯   ◯ **a** are becoming harder to find.

2 Frogs ◯   ◯ **b** are disappearing at a fast rate.

3 Scientists ◯   ◯ **c** did research in Papua New Guinea.

4 New animals ◯   ◯ **d** are working hard to find new plants and animals.

5 Forests ◯   ◯ **e** help keep our environment clean.

VOCABULARY

A **Complete the sentences.** Use the words in the box.

> chase   come across   frequently   get along   injured   survive

1 Animals need air, water, shelter, and food to _____ .

2 If you _____ a sick animal, try to call a vet right away.

3 When an animal is _____ , try not to touch it.

4 My pet cat and dog don't _____ very well.

5 A cheetah can _____ its prey for a kilometer before it gets too tired.

6 Dolphins _____ swim in front of fast-moving boats.

B **Rewrite the sentences.** Use the correct form of the phrasal verbs in the box.

> come across   come along   come back   come up

1 She returned from her vacation last night.

_____ .

2 The plans for the party are progressing.

_____ .

3 Where did you find these photos?

_____ ?

4 Something happened unexpectedly.

_____ .

WRITING

WRITING TIP **USING ADVERBS**

Adverbs add detail to sentences and make them more interesting. You can use them in different ways.

Use adverbs to say how something happens or how someone does something.

The cheetahs ran **quickly**.   They walked **quietly** in the forest.

Use adverbs to say how often something happens or is true.

Owls **often** hunt at night   Dolphins are **usually** gray.

Use adverbs to make adjectives stronger or weaker.

Octopuses are **very** intelligent.   The puppy is **a little** scared.

A Read the article. Notice the adverbs.

Red-eyed tree frogs live in Central America. They **usually** live in ponds, rivers, and trees. They are bright green. This helps them blend in with their surroundings. They also have bright red eyes and orange toes. During the day, the tree frogs sleep **quietly.** They hide under leaves so that other animals can't see them **easily**. But if a bird or snake finds a tree frog, the frog flashes its big red eyes and bright orange toes. This **often** surprises the animal and gives the frog enough time to jump away **quickly** and escape.

B Think about an animal you like. What makes it interesting or unusual? Make notes.

C Write a paragraph. Use your notes from **B**. Include different types of adverbs.

_____

_____

_____

_____

_____

_____

_____

_____

_____

5

I'M MEETING
FRIENDS LATER

PREVIEW

A Complete the phrases. Circle the correct answers.

1 doing **TV** / **sports**

2 listening to **music** / **dinner**

3 browsing the **park** / **internet**

4 watching **TV** / **books**

5 visiting **relatives** / **the internet**

6 having **dinner** / **a movie**

7 playing **TV** / **video games**

8 going for **sports** / **a swim**

B Complete the conversation. Use the words in the box.

> browse   family   jog   mall   meet   movie   read   spend

Kevin: How do you usually ¹ _____ your weekend, Sun-Hee?

Sun-Hee: I usually ² _____ my friend Jessie. We like to exercise, so we often ³ _____ in the park on Saturday morning. Then we go to the ⁴ _____ for pizza.

Kevin: Is that what you're doing this weekend?

Sun-Hee: Actually, no. Jessie's on vacation with her ⁵ _____ this weekend. On Saturday, I'm watching a ⁶ _____ with Alex, and on Sunday, I'm studying for a test. What about you?

Kevin: I'm working on a science project with Lin on Monday, so I think I'm just going to ⁷ _____ the internet and ⁸ _____ a few articles to prepare.

Sun-Hee: Well, I'm studying at the library on Sunday. Why don't you join me?

C Write. What are you doing tonight or tomorrow?

_____

_____

LANGUAGE FOCUS

A Complete the conversation. Circle the correct answers.

Ling: Hey, Sara. What ¹ **are / do** you ² **do / doing** tonight?

Sara: Um ... ³ **I prepare / I'm preparing** for a chemistry test I have on Wednesday.

Ling: Oh, I see. How about later in the week?

Sara: ⁴ **I go / I'm going** to see the new *Star Wars* movie on Friday night. Would you like to come?

Ling: Sure, I'd love to. What time ⁵ **does / is** the movie ⁶ **start / starting**?

Sara: At 7:30 p.m. We can meet outside the movie theater at 7:15.

Ling: Great! I can't wait.

B Correct one mistake in each sentence or question.

1 I'm go cycling with my friends this weekend.   *going*

2 My flight doesn't gets in until midnight.

3 Does the concert starts at 5:30 p.m.?

4 Do you buying the decorations later?

5 She is having a doctor's appointment at 3 o'clock.

6 What time are you meet your friends?

7 When is Sally and Lin's mother arrives tomorrow?

8 Do Pete and Oscar really going to space camp next week?

C Match. Join the two parts of the conversation.

1 Hey, Lara. Are you doing anything interesting this evening? ○   ○ **a** Really? That sounds fun. What time does it start?

2 I'm going to the Harry Styles concert. I have an extra ticket. ○   ○ **b** And I could finish my homework after the concert!

3 Let me check. It starts at 7 p.m. ○   ○ **c** It sure is. See you soon!

4 Around 9:30. Why don't you come? You could be home by 10:00. ○   ○ **d** Not really. I'm staying in and doing my homework. What about you?

5 So, is that a yes? ○   ○ **e** I see. And when does it end?

THE REAL WORLD

The Statue of Liberty was a gift from France to the US.

A Skim the article. Choose the best title.

a   What Inspired Kasha Slavner

b   The Gift from France

c   The First Crowdfunding Project

When Kasha Slavner decided to travel the world and make her documentary, she knew she needed help. She decided to turn to the internet. She started an online crowdfunding project and asked people from around the world to help pay for her trip. Her project was very popular and she soon earned enough money to travel and film for six months!

Crowdfunding may seem like a modern and creative way to raise money, but is it really a new idea? You may be surprised to learn that the first crowdfunding project happened over a hundred years ago!

In 1885, the Statue of Liberty arrived in New York as a gift from France. But New York had a problem. It didn't have enough money to build the statue's $250,000 pedestal—the large area below where the statue stands. To solve the problem, Joseph Pulitzer—a famous newspaper publisher—asked his readers to help pay for the pedestal. In just five months, more than 160,000 people helped raise the money needed to build it. Most gave just a dollar.

Today, the Statue of Liberty stands proudly in New York Harbor—on the same pedestal that the people of New York helped pay for more than a hundred years ago.

B Read the article. Circle **T** for True, **F** for False, or **NG** for Not Given.

1 Kasha Slavner was the first person to use crowdfunding.   **T   F   NG**

2 The Statue of Liberty's pedestal was a gift from France.   **T   F   NG**

3 Joseph Pulitzer asked his newspaper readers for money.   **T   F   NG**

4 It took five months to build the pedestal.   **T   F   NG**

5 The Statue of Liberty now has a new pedestal.   **T   F   NG**

READING

A **Skim the article.** Who is the app for? Check (✓) the correct options.

☐ travelers who want to meet locals

☐ travelers who want to meet other travelers

☐ people who want to reconnect with old friends

COUCHSURFING

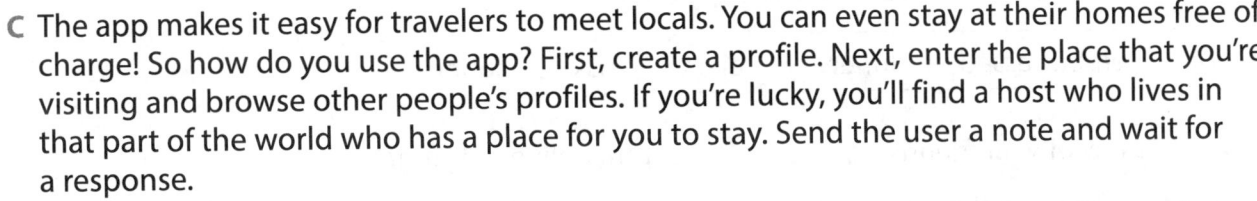

A You arrive in a strange new town and you're all alone. Nobody speaks your language, and there's not much information online about the place you're in. You're ready to explore, but you're not sure what to do. Wouldn't it be nice to know someone local who could help you out or give you some advice?

B One of the best ways to learn about a country is by getting to know its people. Unfortunately, that's not always easy to do. This is where travel apps come in. There are many to choose from, but one of the most popular is Couchsurfing, an app that connects 14 million travelers and hosts from around the world.

C The app makes it easy for travelers to meet locals. You can even stay at their homes free of charge! So how do you use the app? First, create a profile. Next, enter the place that you're visiting and browse other people's profiles. If you're lucky, you'll find a host who lives in that part of the world who has a place for you to stay. Send the user a note and wait for a response.

D But what if you don't need a place to stay? Just use the Hangouts section of the app and look for people near you. You'll find many travelers and locals who are happy to meet up and show you around. Find out what they are doing and join them. Or make your own plans and see who joins you. Either way, it's a great way to meet new people!

B **Answer the questions about *Couchsurfing*.**

1 DETAIL According to the article, what can be difficult to do while traveling?

   a finding cheap rooms   **b** meeting locals   **c** finding good reviews

2 PURPOSE The purpose of paragraph **C** is to show people how to _____.

   a find a place to stay

   b meet locals with similar interests

   c meet travelers to share a place with

3 VOCABULARY If people *show you around* (paragraph **D**), they show you _____.

   a interesting places   **b** ways to meet others   **c** how to do something

4 REFERENCE Who does *they* refer to in paragraph **D**?

    a travelers   **b** local people   **c** travelers and local people

5 DETAIL According to the article, what is true about the Couchsurfing app?

    a It has millions of users.   **b** It lists the best hotels.   **c** It is expensive to use.

C **EXAM PRACTICE** **Read the sentence.** Check (✓) the correct options.

According to the article, the Couchsurfing app _____ .

▢ helps travelers find free places to stay

▢ has audio walking tours for many cities

▢ allows travelers to make friends more easily

▢ contains reviews of popular tourist sites

▢ translates from one language to another

▢ allows users to see what other people are doing

VOCABULARY

A **Complete the conversations.** Use the words in the box.

> accept   embarrassed   lonely   reject   risk   suffer

1 **Pablo:**   Do any of your friends _____ from online bullying?

    Caroline: Lisa does. But she's too _____ to tell anyone about it.

2 **Sarah:**   Moving to California is a big _____ . You don't know anyone there!

    Chris: Don't worry. I won't be _____ for long. I'm good at making friends!

3 **Alex:**   Do you always _____ online friend requests?

    Jon: I usually do. I only _____ people I don't know.

B **Complete the sentences.** Circle the correct answers.

1 It's **surprised / surprising** that so many people stayed home today.

2 I fell asleep halfway through the movie. I was really **bored / boring**.

3 He fell over on stage while accepting his award. It was quite **embarrassed / embarrassing**!

4 I felt **worried / worrying** when my teacher asked me to see her after class.

5 The teacher's instructions were **confused / confusing**, so I asked Elaine for help.

6 He kept talking during the lecture. I found it quite **annoyed / annoying**.

WRITING

WRITING TIP **WRITING AN INFORMAL EMAIL INVITATION**

When writing an informal email invitation, use simple grammar and short sentences to keep the email clear and easy to understand.

A Read the email and information.

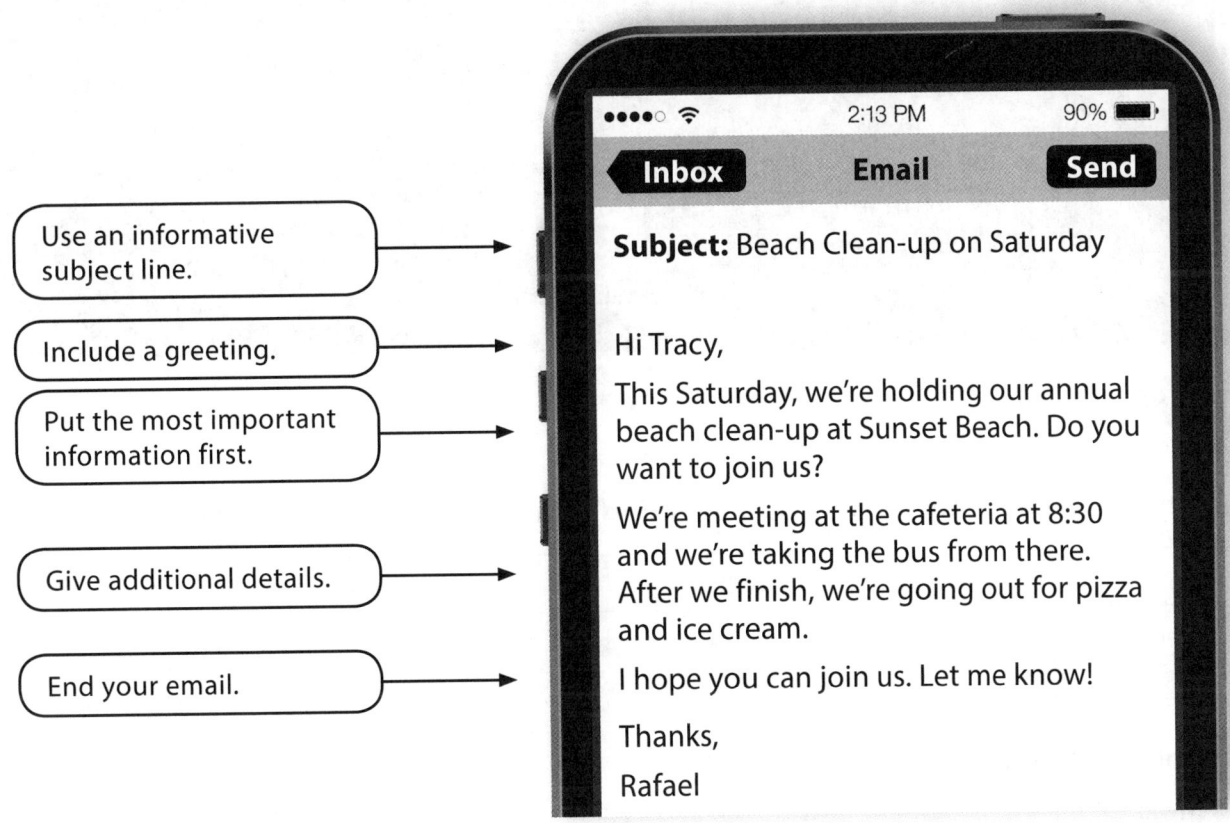

Use an informative subject line.

Include a greeting.

Put the most important information first.

Give additional details.

End your email.

2:13 PM   90%

Inbox   **Email**   **Send**

Subject: Beach Clean-up on Saturday

Hi Tracy,

This Saturday, we're holding our annual beach clean-up at Sunset Beach. Do you want to join us?

We're meeting at the cafeteria at 8:30 and we're taking the bus from there. After we finish, we're going out for pizza and ice cream.

I hope you can join us. Let me know!

Thanks,

Rafael

B Think about something you are doing soon. Who can you invite to join you? What are the most important details? Make notes.

C Write an informal email. Use your notes from **B**. Follow the email organization in **A**.

_____

_____

_____

_____

_____

_____

_____

_____

WHAT WILL EARTH BE LIKE IN THE FUTURE?

PREVIEW

A **What are the possible dangers of global warming?** Check (✓) the correct predictions.

	will rise	will decrease
ocean levels	✓	
the number of animals		
the amount of farmland		
temperatures		
food supplies		

B **Match.** Join the words to make phrases.

1 coral ○   ○ **a** problems

2 environmental ○   ○ **b** cars

3 organic ○   ○ **c** reefs

4 electric ○   ○ **d** food

5 drinking ○   ○ **e** footprint

6 renewable ○   ○ **f** gases

7 carbon ○   ○ **g** energy

8 greenhouse ○   ○ **h** water

C Write. Use words from **A** and **B** to write three predictions about the future.

_____

_____

_____

LANGUAGE FOCUS

A Look at the chart. Complete the sentences below.

WHEN WILL GLOBAL WARMING START TO AFFECT YOU?

19% 34% 20% 13% 14%

0   2   10   25   50   never

Number of years from now

Answered by 2,129 Americans.

1 _____ people took the survey.

2 About _____ percent of the people who took the survey think global warming will never affect them.

3 About 34 percent of the people in the survey think global warming will start affecting them **5 / 10 / 25** years from now.

4 About **53 / 73 / 86** percent of the people who took the survey think that global warming will affect us less than 50 years from now.

B Complete the sentences. Use the words _fewer_ or _less_.

1 In the future, there will probably be _____ oil.

2 I think in the next 50 years, people will have _____ children.

3 If the ice melts, there will be _____ polar bears in the Arctic.

4 When I get a job, I will have _____ free time than now.

5 I think there will be _____ environmental problems in the future.

6 We have to use _____ energy if we want to reduce our carbon footprint.

C Complete the conversation. Number the sentences in the correct order.

a _____ I don't know. Some us may need to find new homes in space! We really should do something to stop global warming while we can.

b _____ Hmm. What kind of problems?

c _____ 34°C? I can't remember the last time it was that hot.

d _____ It sure is. And if we don't do something about it now, we'll have big problems in the future.

e __1__ Did you read the news? The temperature tomorrow afternoon will be 34°C.

f _____ Well, if it gets too hot, Arctic ice will melt. Ocean levels will rise and there'll be less land.

g _____ Me neither. I wonder. Is global warming starting to affect us already?

h _____ Oh no. Will there be enough land for everyone to live on?

THE REAL WORLD

A melting glacier in Norway

In his book *Six Degrees*, Mark Lynas describes what will happen when Earth's temperatures increase up to six degrees.

With a four-degree temperature increase, all Arctic ice will melt and disappear for the first time in three million years. This means that polar bears and other Arctic mammals could die out.

If temperatures increase by five degrees, the ice in Antarctica will melt more quickly. Eventually, it will disappear completely. In other words, there won't be any ice in either the South or North Poles. Also, ocean temperatures will rise, which will wipe out coral reefs.

With a six-degree temperature rise, sea levels will go up by two meters, threatening all major cities near the coast. Humans may survive, but many other species on Earth will face extinction.

Global warming is a serious problem, but by changing our lifestyles and using less fossil fuel, we can save our planet before it is too late.

A **Match.** What will happen when Earth's temperature increases by 4, 5, or 6 degrees Celsius?

1 4°C ○   ○ **a** Ice on both the North and South Poles will disappear.

2 5°C ○   ○ **b** Rising oceans will threaten all major coastal cities.

3 6°C ○   ○ **c** Arctic animals will be in danger of extinction.

B **Read the sentences.** Circle **T** for True or **F** for False.

1 The last time Arctic ice disappeared was three million years ago.   **T**   **F**

2 The ice in Antarctica will disappear before Arctic ice.   **T**   **F**

3 Rising ocean levels are a bigger problem for cities near the coast.   **T**   **F**

READING

A Skim the article. Circle the correct answer.

Carbon dioxide capture and storage will help to capture CO_2 released from _____.

a houses and cars
b farms
c power plants

MAKING POWER PLANTS GREEN

A power plant and CO_2 truck

Carbon dioxide (CO_2) is a greenhouse gas that occurs naturally in the atmosphere. But when humans burn fossil fuels to create electricity, we increase the amount of CO_2 in the atmosphere. This causes global warming. But some scientists believe they
5 have a solution. They are developing ways to capture the CO_2 released from power plants and store it underground. This technique is called carbon dioxide capture and storage (CCS).

So how does CCS work? Most power plants produce carbon dioxide. But CCS power plants trap the CO_2 they produce
10 before it escapes into the atmosphere. They then transport the carbon away—usually by pipeline, but also by trucks or ships. Pipelines then send the CO_2 underground to be stored safely and permanently in rock formations. Once it is underground, CCS plants check the area regularly to make sure there are
15 no CO_2 leaks.

Currently, there are more than 20 CCS plants around the world. Together, they capture more than 30 million tons of CO_2 every year. CCS plants can actually sell some of this CO_2 to other factories that make things like housing materials, medicines, perfumes, and even sodas. This means that the number of plants will definitely increase as more companies try
20 to make money from carbon.

Carbon-capture technology is still developing—we will probably have to wait many years before we can use it on a large scale. However, in the long run, CCS could help decrease CO_2 in a way that actually makes money. This can only be good news in the fight to stop global warming.

B Answer the questions about *Making Power Plants Green*.

1 MAIN IDEA CO_2 is increasing in the atmosphere because of _____.

   a plants and animals
   b human activity
   c temperature changes

2 VOCABULARY *Capture* in line 5 means _____.

   a catch
   b waste
   c make

3 DETAIL Most of the CO_2 that a CCS power plant produces will be _____.

   a stored underground
   b sold to factories
   c released into the atmosphere

4 INFERENCE Scientists are probably most concerned about the safety of _____ .

    a reusing CO_2 **b** transporting CO_2 **c** storing CO_2

5 INFERENCE The writer thinks that carbon-capture technology will _____ .

    a soon be used commercially   **b** be unprofitable   **c** help stop global warming

C **EXAM PRACTICE** **Look at the diagram.** Answer the questions about the different stages of the CCS process. Use words from the article.

1 CCS plants _____ carbon dioxide before it _____ into the atmosphere.

2 Trucks, pipelines, or ships _____ the carbon away.

3 Pipelines send the CO_2 _____ where it is stored in rock formations.

4 Plant workers _____ the area regularly to make sure there are no _____ .

VOCABULARY

A **Match.** Join the words and phrases to their meanings.

  1 a cracked cup   ◯   ◯ **a** an important part of a job

  2 a creature   ◯   ◯ **b** one that could become extinct

  3 a drowning person   ◯   ◯ **c** someone that you know from the past

  4 an endangered species ◯   ◯ **d** one that's damaged but not completely broken

  5 a familiar face   ◯   ◯ **e** someone who is underwater and can't breathe

  6 a vital role   ◯   ◯ **f** an animal, or a monster in a story

B **Complete the sentences.** Use the words in the box.

> cloudy   icy   itchy   lucky   muddy   noisy

1 You should be careful when driving in the winter on _____ roads.

2 The weather was _____ and not too hot.

3 My arm touched that plant, and now it's really _____ . I can't stop scratching!

4 The soccer field usually turns _____ after a rainy day.

5 He was in a terrible accident. He's _____ to be alive.

6 I'm trying to do my homework, but the party downstairs is too _____.

WRITING

WRITING TIP **USING ADVERBS TO SHOW CERTAINTY**

Show readers how certain you are by using the adverbs **probably** and **definitely**.

A **Look at the chart.** Then read the paragraph and underline the adverbs that show certainty.

In the next 10 to 20 years, . . .			
most homes	will **probably** / **probably** won't will / won't will **definitely** / **definitely** won't	use solar energy.	less certain ↕ more certain

In the next 20 years, most homes in the US will probably use solar energy. Today, solar panels are expensive, but many new homes already use them to create electricity. In the future, solar panels will definitely become cheaper. They will also probably be better at making electricity. Therefore, many more people will use them.

B **Think of a technology you are interested in.** How do you think that technology will change in the future? Make notes.

C **Write a paragraph.** Use your notes from **B**. Include adverbs to show how certain you are.

_____

_____

_____

_____

_____

_____

_____

_____

WHEN DID IT HAPPEN?

PREVIEW

A Complete the sentences. Use the words in the box.

> China   mammoth   Olympic   pyramid   Wall

1 The ancient Egyptians built their first _____ more than 4,600 years ago.

2 The woolly _____ became extinct in 1650 B.C.

3 The first ancient _____ Games were in 776 B.C.

4 Marco Polo reached _____ in A.D. 1275.

5 China began building the Great _____ in 221 B.C.

B Match. Join the two parts of the sentences.

1 Cleopatra ruled Egypt for ⟶ ○   ○ **a** to 1865.

2 Mark Zuckerberg formed Facebook in ○   ○ **b** 22 years.

3 Abraham Lincoln was the US president from 1861 ○   ○ **c** January 1, 2017.

4 People began speaking English more than ○   ○ **d** 2004.

5 António Guterres became the UN Secretary General on ○   ○ **e** 1,500 years ago.

C Write. Think of an important world event. When did it happen and how long did it last?

_____

LANGUAGE FOCUS

A **Complete the conversation.** Use the words in the box.

> ago   did   for   from
> on   to   was   were

Tim: Mom, when ¹ _____ you and dad first meet?

Ellen: We met more than 20 years ² _____ . We were in college.

Tim: Wow! And when ³ _____ your wedding?

Ellen: We got married ⁴ _____ July 24th, 1994.

Tim: Hmm ... So how long did you date before getting married?

Ellen: Let's see. I think we dated ⁵ _____ about 5 years.

Tim: Cool. Where did you go for your honeymoon?

Ellen: We went to Costa Rica. We stayed by the beach.

Tim: That's nice. How long ⁶ _____ you there?

Ellen: We were there ⁷ _____ August ⁸ _____ September. We had a great time!

B **Correct one mistake in each sentence or question.**

1 Mickey Mouse first appeared ~~on~~ *in* 1928.

2 How long ago was you visit Scotland?

3 When did the first modern Olympic Games took place?

4 How ago did the *Titanic* sink?

5 When did the first 3-D movie?

6 Amelia Earhart disappeared in July 2, 1937.

C **Complete the conversation.** Number the sentences in the correct order.

_____ I need some information on Abraham Lincoln. When was he president of the United States?

_____ So he was president for four years. Thanks! And how did he die?

_1_ Hey, Kim. Do you have a minute? I need help with my history homework.

_____ Oh, yeah. I remember now. He died while he was still President. How old was he?

_____ Sure. How can I help?

_____ You should know this! A man named John Wilkes Booth shot him in a theater.

_____ He was only 56. He died more than 150 years ago, but many people still remember him today for all the important things he did.

_____ Hmm ... Let me check online. It says here that he was president from 1861 to 1865.

THE **FIRST** SATELLITES

A Soviet scientist works on the first Sputnik satellite.

A Skim the article. Number the satellites in the order they were launched.

a _____ Explorer 1   b _____ Sputnik   c _____ Sputnik 2   d _____ Vanguard TV3

On October 4, 1957, the Soviet Union launched Sputnik, the first human-made satellite, into space. This historic event surprised the world and started a decade-long space race with the United States.

Sputnik was a small, round object. It was only about 60 centimeters wide, but because it was shiny, people on Earth could see it flying through the sky. It moved quickly, too, orbiting Earth at 29,000 kilometers per hour. The satellite sent signals back to Earth for 22 days before its batteries died, and it stayed in space for three months before falling back to Earth.

But Sputnik wasn't the only satellite the Soviets launched in 1957. On November 3, they sent Sputnik 2 into space. The US responded. On December 6, 1957, they tried to launch their own satellite—the Vanguard TV3—but failed. Finally, on February 1, 1958, the US succeeded with the launch of Explorer 1.

B Read the article. Circle the correct answers.

1 What is true about the space race?

   a It lasted for two years.   b The US started it.   c It started over 60 years ago.

2 People on Earth could see Sputnik in the sky because it was _____.

   a round   b shiny   c fast

3 Sputnik fell back to Earth _____.

   a after three months   b after 22 days   c when its batteries died

4 In 1958, the US _____.

   a launched Sputnik 2   b failed to launch a satellite   c put a satellite into space

READING

A Skim the article. The article is mainly about Battuta's _____.

a visit to Mecca   **b** adventures   **c** character

THE TRAVELS OF IBN BATTUTA

You probably know about Marco Polo, the famous Italian explorer of the 13th century. But do you know about Ibn Battuta? Ibn Battuta was a great explorer from Morocco who started traveling around the time that Marco Polo died.

Ibn Battuta meets a king in India.

5 Battuta left his home in Tangier in 1325, when he was 21 years old. He set off for Mecca and continued traveling for nearly 30 years. He visited what today would be 44 countries in Asia and Africa. His travels weren't always easy. Once, bandits attacked and nearly killed him. Another time, after setting sail from Sri Lanka, his ship sank. But despite the difficulties he faced, Battuta saw many amazing things. In India, for example, he went to a

10 palace and met a king who had 200 soldiers, 60 horses, and 50 elephants protecting him. The elephants were all wearing real gold.

Battuta's last journey was in 1352, to the West African kingdom of Mali. Mali was a rich kingdom famous for its gold. There were many stories about its generous king who gave his guests wonderful gifts, like gold and clothes made of fine silk. It took Battuta more than

15 two months to cross the Sahara Desert and reach Mali. However, when he finally got there, there was a new king. The gifts he received were not what he expected—three loaves of bread, fried beef, and some yogurt!

When Battuta finally returned to Morocco, he wrote a book about his adventures. Many people read his book and translated it into different languages. Because of this, we now

20 know much about Battuta's life and the world during the 14th century.

B Answer the questions about *The Travels of Ibn Battuta*.

1 INFERENCE Why does the writer say "what today would be 44 countries"?

  a The number of countries was different in the 14th century.

  b The stories of Battuta's travels were mostly made up.

  c Battuta actually visited much fewer than 44 countries.

2 PURPOSE The purpose of the second paragraph is to describe the _____ of Battuta's travels.

  a best parts   **b** worst parts   **c** highlights

3 VOCABULARY The word *bandits* in line 7 refers to people who _____.

  a help guide people   **b** give food to travelers   **c** steal from people

4 DETAIL Ibn Battuta _____ from the king of Mali.

  a expected to receive better gifts

  b didn't expect to receive any gifts

  c was surprised to receive expensive gifts

5 DETAIL Which of the following is NOT true about Ibn Battuta's book?

    a Historians used it to learn about the 14th century.

    b Battuta wrote it in many different languages.

    c People of different cultures have read it.

C EXAM PRACTICE **Write.** Add the events (**a–f**) to the timeline.

    a Ibn Battuta crosses the Sahara.   **d** Ibn Battuta writes a book.

    b Ibn Battuta meets an Indian king.   **e** Ibn Battuta returns home.

    c Ibn Battuta leaves Tangier.   **f** Ibn Battuta arrives in Mali.

1 _____	2 _____	3 _____	4 _____	5 _____	6 _____

VOCABULARY

A **Complete the paragraph.** Use the correct form of the words in the box.

> belong   bury   clue   escape   theory   valuable

In 2014, a couple in California, USA, noticed an old can sticking out of a hill on their property. What they found inside was very [1] _____—10 million dollars in gold coins! Who did the coins [2] _____ to? Nobody knows, but one important [3] _____ is their dates: 1847 to 1890. This is around the time of the California Gold Rush, when more than 300,000 people came to California to look for gold. One [4] _____ is that the owner [5] _____ the coins because they didn't trust banks. Another is that bandits hid it while trying to [6] _____ from the law.

B **Complete the sentences.** Use the correct form of the words in the box.

> chopsticks   copper   gadget   sword
> laptop   material   utensil   weapon

    1 The piece of metal came from a sharp _____, like a knife or a _____.

    2 People around the world eat with different _____, like _____ or forks.

    3 One _____ that ancient people used to make tools was _____.

    4 We all use _____ to communicate, like cell phones or _____.

WRITING

WRITING TIP **ORGANIZING DETAILS CHRONOLOGICALLY**

When writing about an event, it sometimes helps to list details chronologically, or in the order they happened. Use time words like the ones in the box below to help you.

in	after	during
later	when	finally

A **Read the paragraph.** Then underline the time words in the paragraph.

Ibn Battuta was born in 1304. He grew up in Morocco and studied law. In 1325, Battuta left home to see the world. He visited many places during his travels. He also faced many troubles. For example, bandits robbed him. And later, pirates attacked his ship. Battuta's last trip was to Mali. When he arrived in Mali, the king welcomed him with gifts of food. After visiting Mali, Battuta finally went home. He was 49 years old. Later, he wrote a book about his amazing travels.

B **Think of an important historical event.** Research the event and list the details of the event in chronological order.

C **Write a paragraph.** Use your notes from **B**. Use the different time words in **A**.

_____

_____

_____

_____

_____

_____

_____

_____

_____

_____

_____

_____

HAVE YOU EVER TRIED GO-KARTING?

PREVIEW

A Match. Join the pictures and the words.

1  ○ ○ **a** parasailing

2  ○ ○ **b** bungee jumping

3  ○ ○ **c** horseback riding

4  ○ ○ **d** go-karting

5  ○ ○ **e** sandboarding

6  ○ ○ **f** skydiving

7  ○ ○ **g** zip-lining

8  ○ ○ **h** hot-air ballooning

B Complete the sentences. Use the activities from **A**.

1 I don't think I want to try _____. I'm afraid of large animals.

2 _____ from one tree to another is a great way to experience the jungle.

3 _____ looks really scary. I can't imagine jumping out of an airplane.

4 _____ was fun, but it was also tiring. The desert was really hot.

5 I've never driven before, but I'm going to try _____ this weekend.

C Write. Which two activities in **A** do you think are the most dangerous? Why?

_____

_____

LANGUAGE FOCUS

A Complete the sentences. Use the correct form of the words in parentheses.

1 I've never _____ (**play**) basketball in my life.

2 Have you ever _____ (**drink**) watermelon juice?

3 Have you ever _____ (**see**) an elephant?

4 I haven't _____ (**be**) to this mall before.

5 She's never _____ (**have**) a surprise party.

B Complete the conversations. Use the correct form of the verbs in parentheses.

1 A: _____ you ever _____ a password before? (**forget**)

   B: No, I _____. I'm pretty good at remembering them.

2 C: _____ she ever _____ to New Zealand? (**be**)

   D: No, she _____. But she's going next month.

3 E: _____ you _____ this movie before? (**see**)

   F: Yes, I _____. I've _____ it many times, actually. (**watch**)

4 G: How many times _____ you _____ them? (**meet**)

   H: Just once. But I've _____ with them many times on the phone. (**speak**)

5 I: I _____ on TV before. (**never appear**)

   J: Neither _____ I. But I _____ on stage a few times. (**sing**)

6 K: Geena and Stacy _____ hiking before. What about you? (**never go**)

   L: No, we _____ either. But we think it will be fun!

C Match. Join the two parts of the conversation.

1 When does summer break start? ○
   I'm thinking of taking a vacation.

2 I'm not sure. But I'd like to go ○
   somewhere in Latin America.

3 I've been there twice. You're right ○
   about the museums, but I think
   I'd prefer to be closer to the sea.

4 No, I haven't, but I've always ○
   wanted to visit. Now, all I need is
   someone to come with me.

○ a Well, I haven't been there, either.
       Why don't we go together?

○ b It starts next month. Where are
       you planning to go?

○ c Yeah, Mexico City doesn't
       have any beaches. Have you ever
       been to Costa Rica?

○ d How about Mexico City?
       Have you ever been? It has
       some excellent museums.

LA TOMATINA

La Tomatina is one of Europe's most popular festivals.

A Scan the article. What are the two rules of the festival?

1 You can't _____.

2 You have to _____.

Have you ever been in a food fight? If you haven't, think about visiting Spain. Every year, on the last Wednesday of August, the tiny town of Buñol holds the *La Tomatina* festival. It's the world's largest food fight, with thousands of people throwing tomatoes at each other, just for fun!

The event starts at 10 a.m. A large piece of meat is placed at the end of a long piece of wood that's covered in oil, and people have to try to climb up to get it. As soon as someone grabs the piece of meat, the food fight begins. The rules are simple. First, don't throw anything that's not a tomato. And second, crush your tomatoes to soften them before throwing them—a hard, unsqueezed tomato to the head can be quite painful! The festival continues until about 11 a.m. By the time it's over, the streets and everyone on them are completely covered in tomato juice.

Hugo has taken part in *La Tomatina* more than 20 times. He has seen it grow from a small local event to a much larger one. In 2012, about 50,000 people took part! The year after, the town of Buñol decided to limit the number of people who could take part to 20,000 per year.

B Read the article. Circle the correct answers.

1 People throw tomatoes at each other as a way to **have fun** / **win an argument**.

2 The long piece of wood is difficult to climb because it is very **hot** / **oily**.

3 The *La Tomatina* festival goes on for about **one hour** / **one day**.

4 Hugo has **organized** / **participated in** many *La Tomatina* festivals.

5 About **20,000** / **50,000** people attended the *La Tomatina* festival in 2013.

READING

AN AFRICAN ADVENTURE

A **Skim the text.** Where is Amelia, and who is she with?

_____

To:	Paul		Subject:	Kenya

Hi Paul,

I can't believe I'm finally here—I've always wanted to go on a safari! And I can't wait for you and your parents to join us. We're going to have so much fun together.

5   So far, this trip has been both good and bad. The flight to Kenya was the longest I've ever been on—it was really tiring. Also, when we arrived at the airport in Kenya, we couldn't find our bags. We later found out that they were mixed up with the bags from another flight. It took us more than two hours to get our luggage!

10   But later that day, things got better. We went to a local market, and my Mom and I tried *ugali*. It's a traditional Kenyan dish made of corn. It was delicious! You should try it when you get here. My dad was less adventurous. He ate banana pancakes just like the ones we usually have at the café back home!

The next day, we started our safari in a place called Maasai Mara. That's where we are now.
15   My mom has taken about a thousand photos! We saw so many animals, including giraffes, zebras, elephants, and crocodiles. I even saw a lion, but no one believes me. ☹

Anyway, I can't wait to see you. I've written a list of things for us to do together, including horseback riding. It'll be so much fun!

Write back soon.
20   Amelia

B **Answer the questions about *An African Adventure*.**

1   MAIN IDEA   The email is mainly about Amelia's _____.
   a flight and hotel   **b** trip to Maasai Mara   **c** trip so far

2   INFERENCE   Has Amelia ever flown in an airplane before?
   a Yes, she has.   **b** No, she hasn't.   **c** We don't know.

3   DETAIL   *Ugali* (line 11) is the name of _____.
   a a local market   **b** a type of food   **c** a type of plant

4 DETAIL Why was Amelia's father less adventurous?

    a He ate something familiar.

    b He didn't go to the market.

    c He didn't enjoy the taste of *ugali*.

5 INFERENCE What hasn't Amelia done on her trip yet?

    a been on a safari   **b** gone horseback riding   **c** made a list of things to do

C EXAM PRACTICE **Read the article again.** Check (✓) all the people who did each thing.

	Amelia	Amelia's mother	Amelia's father
lost luggage			
tried ugali			
went on a safari			
took about a thousand photos			
saw zebras and crocodiles			
saw a lion			

VOCABULARY

A **Complete the sentences.** Use the words in the box.

> balance   essentially   lifetime   personal   remind   worthwhile

1 It's not always easy to _____ work and play these days.

2 My vacation to New Zealand really was the trip of a(n) _____.

3 I think that working as a teacher would be a(n) _____ career.

4 What the book says about São Paulo is _____ true.

5 He didn't say why he couldn't make it. He said his reasons were _____.

6 Please _____ me when you are coming to visit.

B **Complete the sentences.** Circle the correct answers.

1 Have you ever **done** / **played** golf?

2 My brothers want to **go** / **play** windsurfing, but there's no wind!

3 My sister goes dancing a lot, but she has never **gone** / **done** ballet.

4 I hope to **go** / **take** traveling in Southeast Asia after I graduate.

5 If you want to **do** / **take** better photos, try **going** / **taking** a class.

6 When he's not **doing** / **playing** professional soccer, he's **doing** / **taking** something worthwhile.

WRITING

WRITING TIP **USING THE PRESENT PERFECT AND SIMPLE PAST**

The present perfect is useful for talking about things that people have experienced. We often use the simple past to expand on these experiences and add details.

> Use the present perfect to describe things you have done:
>
> **I've been skydiving seven times.**
>
> Use the simple past to add specific details:
>
> **I first went skydiving five years ago.**

A Read the paragraph. Circle the present perfect. Underline the simple past.

I've lived in Colorado for many years. My family **moved** here when I was 12 years old. Before that, I **lived** in a small village in Mexico. When I **moved** to the US, I **didn't speak** English. But I **worked** hard at school and **picked up** the language quickly. Since then, **I've visited** several other US states, including Arizona, Utah, and Texas. Last year, I **went** to California for the first time with my parents. We **visited** Hollywood, Disneyland, and Universal Studios.

B Choose one of these topics. Think of several examples and supporting details. Make notes.

- amazing places you have visited
- interesting festivals you have been to
- memorable experiences you have had

C Write a paragraph. Use your notes from **B**. Use both the present perfect and the simple past.

_____

_____

_____

_____

_____

_____

_____

_____

9

PHONES **USED TO BE** MUCH BIGGER!

PREVIEW

A **Match.** Join the two parts of the phrases.

1 chat ○ ○ **a** letters

2 use ○ ○ **b** social media

3 write ○ ○ **c** calls

4 make ○ ○ **d** online

B **Complete the sentences.** Circle the correct answers.

1 Some people don't worry about their spelling when they **text** / **call**.

2 He **emailed** / **chatted** me last night, but he forgot to attach the files.

3 I often **chat** / **text** with people online about sports and video games.

4 You need a pen and paper to **chat online** / **write a letter**.

5 He **writes letters** / **uses social media** a lot. He has many followers online.

6 If you want to speak with someone directly, it's best to **call** / **text**.

C **Write.** Choose three people you know. How do they like to communicate with you?

_____

_____

_____

LANGUAGE FOCUS

A Complete the sentences. Circle the correct answers.

1 I **used to** / **didn't use to** play soccer, but now I play it all the time.

2 Pete **used to** / **never used to** hang out with Paulo, but now they go everywhere together.

3 Ling **used to** / **didn't use to** live in China. Now, she lives in the U.S.

4 I **used to** / **didn't use to** wear a uniform to school. Now, I can wear my own clothes.

5 Prices have gone up in this café. It **used to** / **didn't use to** be so expensive.

6 I **used to** / **didn't use to** live close to my school. Now, I'm just a short distance away.

B Complete the conversations. Use the correct form of *used to*.

1 **A:** Did Laura _____ live in New York.

   B: No, she _____ . She _____ live in Chicago.

2 **C:** Brian never _____ shop here.

   D: Oh, really? Where did he _____ shop?

3 **E:** Why did you _____ like coming here? The food is terrible!

   F: Well, it didn't _____ be so bad.

4 **G:** Did Aisha _____ come here often?

   H: Yes, she _____ . She _____ love going to the comic book store.

5 **I:** What did you _____ do in the past when you were bored?

   J: I _____ read a lot. I never _____ play video games.

C Complete the conversation. Put the sentences in the correct order.

__1__ Hey Kim. Can I ask you some questions about your childhood for a homework assignment?

_____ Well, Korean, of course. And Mandarin. I used to speak some French, but I've forgotten most of it.

_____ No, I didn't. I used to live in Korea. And after Korea, I lived in China for a while.

_____ Sure, Tom. What do you want to know?

_____ You didn't speak English? That must have been tough! What other languages do you speak?

_____ Well, for starters, did you always live in the US?

_____ When I was ten. It was strange moving here. I didn't use to speak English back then.

_____ Cool! And when did you move to the US?

THE RETURN OF VINYL

A collection of vinyl records

A **Skim the article.** Underline all the things that were bad about vinyl records.

Before MP3s and music streaming, people used to buy CDs. Before that, they bought cassettes. Go back a little further and you'll enter the age of vinyl. From the 1950s to the 1980s, when people bought music, they bought vinyl records.

Today, vinyl is becoming popular again. But why? There was a lot wrong with records. They were huge and scratched easily. They couldn't hold many songs. And you had to turn them over halfway through an album.

The main reason records are becoming popular again is nostalgia. Some people want their music to sound the way it used to when they were younger—including all the pops and noises a record player produces! They want to flip through their record collections and enjoy the artwork on the covers, the way they used to in the past.

This "feel-good" effect is why many are returning to vinyl. It is also why some younger people—who never used to listen to vinyl—are starting to collect records. Vinyl sales are growing, and music companies are noticing. One company, Sony, even decided to start producing new records again—their first since 1989!

B **Read the article.** Answer the questions.

1 Number the items in order, from oldest (1) to newest (4).

_____ cassettes _____ vinyl records _____ streaming _____ CDs

2 What is NOT mentioned as a disadvantage of records?

   a they were big   **b** they cost a lot   **c** they got damaged easily

3 *Nostalgia* is a(n) _____ feeling about the past.

   a incorrect   **b** positive   **c** negative

4 According to the article, sales of records are _____ .

   a starting to drop   **b** higher than MP3 sales   **c** continuing to grow

READING

A Skim the article. Label the two devices in the photos.

a

b

AHEAD OF THEIR TIME

Technology has come a long way over the years. But did you know that many of today's technologies were inspired by ideas people had many years ago? Here are three examples.

5 In 1964, the American company AT&T produced a device called the Picturephone. It was essentially a black-and-white TV, a video camera, and a telephone put together. Although the first ever video call was a success, the Picturephone never took off—it was too big and expensive. However, it did show the world that video communication was possible, and it paved the way for webcams and smartphone cameras.

10 In 1968, Alan Kay, a computer scientist, developed an idea for a computer. He called it the Dynabook. Computers back then used to be huge, but Kay wanted the Dynabook to be lightweight and easy to carry around. But because the technology wasn't available at the time, Kay never actually made the Dynabook. He did, however, make a model. His design inspired many computer developers, and finally led to the invention of the modern-day tablet.

15 In the 1970s, inventor Steve Mann came up with the idea of wearable technology. One of his first inventions was the EyeTap Digital Eye Glass—eyeglasses with computer technology built into them. His invention did not take off. People didn't use to own computers, and the idea of wearing one seemed strange. But the idea of wearable technology stuck around, and today more people are starting to wear smart devices.

B Answer the questions about *Ahead of Their Time*.

1 MAIN IDEA What is the main idea of the article?

   a Many of the unsuccessful ideas of the past were too expensive.

   b Many of today's ideas won't be successful until some time in the future.

   c Many of today's products are based on ideas thought of years ago.

2 DETAIL What is NOT true about the AT&T Picturephone?

    a It was very large.   **b** It included a telephone.   **c** Its image was in color.

3 VOCABULARY If a product *paved the way* (line 9) for something else, it _____ .

    a replaced it   **b** made it possible   **c** stopped it from being made

4 DETAIL Alan Kay never actually made the Dynabook because _____ .

    a the design was bad   **b** it weighed too much   **c** the technology didn't exist

5 DETAIL Why didn't people want to wear the EyeTap Digital Eye Glass?

    a It was uncomfortable.   **b** It felt strange.   **c** It was dangerous.

C **EXAM PRACTICE** **What does the article say about the inventions?** Write the letters (**a–f**) in the Venn diagram.

    a was made by a large company

    b was too expensive

    c inspired today's tablet

    d was not commercially successful

    e involved wearing an item

    f was developed in the 1960s

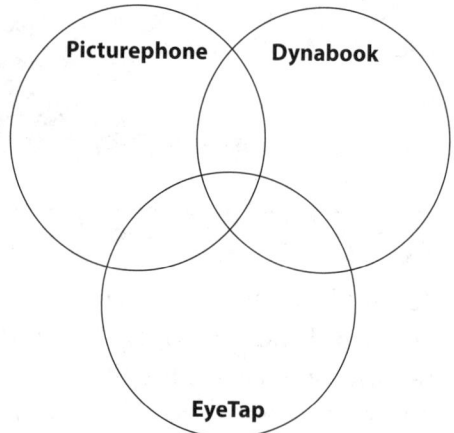

VOCABULARY

A **Complete the conversations.** Use the words in the box.

> available   device   disappear   enormous   replace   store

1 **Adam:** I really don't like this ¹ _____ . It weighs too much.

    Kurt: Why don't you ² _____ it with a lighter one?

2 **Lacey:** Why did floppy disks ³ _____ ?

    Jie-Hae: Because they couldn't ⁴ _____ much information.

3 **Marco:** Computers from the 1960s were ⁵ _____ !

    Bianca: Yeah. The technology for small computers wasn't ⁶ _____ back then.

B **Complete the sentences.** Circle the correct answers.

1 If you're sure you'll never need these files again, **save** / **delete** them.

2 It sometimes takes a while to **back up** / **download** video files from this website.

3 My computer automatically **downloads** / **saves** the changes I make to this presentation every few minutes.

4 You should **back up** / **delete** your files online. Saving them on your computer isn't enough.

WRITING

WRITING TIP **STARTING A STORY**

Start your story with a hook to get the reader interested and wanting to read more.

A Read the information and the model paragraph. What hook does the writer use?

    a an interesting question   **b** an interesting fact   **c** an exciting part

START YOUR STORY WITH:

An interesting question
Do you remember the games you used to play when you were a child?

An interesting fact
More than two-thirds of teenagers say they like dogs more than cats. But that's not true for me. I used to have a pet dog. He was nothing but trouble!

An exciting part of the story
I stood on the stage and looked at the camera. I couldn't move. The audience watched silently, waiting for me to speak.

> Have you ever posted a video of yourself doing something silly online? I have—many times! My friends and I used to pretend to sing along to different songs, and after a while, we started to record videos of ourselves. We used to just laugh and delete the videos, but later, we got more serious about it. We practiced until we were really good, and we posted our videos online for our friends to see. Sometimes, we even wore costumes!

B Think of something that you used to do, but don't do now. Make notes. Write down an interesting question or fact related to your story, or highlight an exciting part.

C Write a story. Use your notes from **B**. Use an interesting hook to engage the reader.

_____

_____

_____

_____

_____

_____

_____

_____

_____

THEY'VE MADE AN AMAZING DISCOVERY!

PREVIEW

A Match. Join the words to their definitions.

1 fossil ○   ○ **a** a large meat-eating dinosaur

2 paleontologist ○   ○ **b** someone who studies old plant and animal remains

3 *T. rex* ○   ○ **c** the remains of a plant or animal preserved in stone

B Read the news story. Then write the letters (**a–f**) on the timeline.

> **PALEONTOLOGIST DISCOVERS *T. REX* RELATIVE**
>
> **a** Paleontologist Lindsay Zanno found a dinosaur fossil back in 2013.
>
> **b** In 2019, paleontologists realized that the fossil belonged to a new species.
>
> **c** Scientists learned in 2016 that the dinosaur was about seven years old.
>
> **d** The small, deer-sized *T. rex* relative lived about 95 million years ago.
>
> **e** The *T. rex*, its much larger cousin, first appeared 85 million years ago.
>
> **f** Paleontologist Barnum Brown discovered the first *T. rex* fossil in 1900.

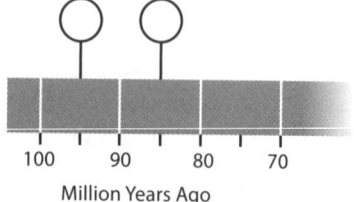

100 90 80 70
Million Years Ago

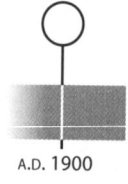

A.D. 1900

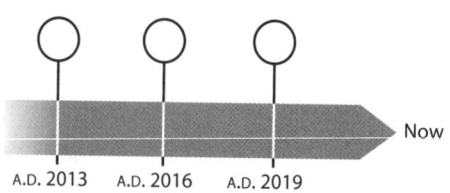

A.D. 2013 A.D. 2016 A.D. 2019   Now

C Write. Summarize Zanno's discovery in two sentences.

_____

_____

_____

LANGUAGE FOCUS

A Complete the conversations. Circle the correct answers.

1 Gina: How long [1] **were you** / **have you been** here?

   Trent: Not long. I [2] **got** / **'ve gotten** here a few minutes ago.

2 Masao: [3] **Did you watch** / **have you watched** the soccer match last night?

   Natalia: No, I [4] **missed** / **'ve missed** it. I fell asleep.

3 Erin: [5] **Did you see** / **Have you seen** Oksana anywhere?

   Walt: I [6] **didn't see** / **haven't seen** her all day.

B Complete the sentences. Use the words _for_ or _since_.

1 John is coming home tomorrow. He's been away _____ years.

2 I haven't eaten in this restaurant _____ my birthday party.

3 Pietro has been waiting for the nurse to call his number _____ noon.

4 I've wanted to join this team _____ a long time.

5 I haven't climbed a tree _____ I was a child.

6 He hasn't seen his family _____ he left home for college.

C Complete the conversation. Number the sentences in the correct order.

a _____ I guess, but I've become much more interested recently, since I started learning Mandarin.

b _____ And you got it! Have you decided on your major?

c _____ Thanks. I got accepted to the university last year, but I didn't think I could afford it. So
        I applied for a scholarship a few months ago.

d __1__ Hey, Lex, are you still planning on going to Cranston College?

e _____ How interesting! Have you always been interested in Asia?

f _____ Yes, I have. I'm going to study Asian History.

g _____ No. Haven't you heard? I've gotten a scholarship to State University.

h _____ Really? That's fantastic. Congratulations!

STORMQUAKES

A photograph of Hurricane Florence taken from space

A **Scan the article.** Choose the best definition of a stormquake.

a the shaking of the ocean floor caused by a storm

b the shaking of ocean water caused by an earthquake

c the shaking caused when an earthquake hits during a storm

Scientists have discovered that sometimes the ocean floor shakes during a powerful storm. They have called this event a "stormquake." The shaking can be as strong as a small earthquake. It can last for days and be spread out over thousands of kilometers.

So what causes stormquakes? Powerful storms often create giant waves out in the sea, and the effects of these waves sometimes travel all the way down to the ocean floor. When the waves are big enough, the ocean floor shakes. But this only happens if the ocean floor is shaped a certain way.

Fan Wenyuan is a scientist from Florida State University who studies stormquakes. Over a 10-year period, his team recorded nearly 15,000 stormquakes. These underwater events are actually fairly common. Luckily, despite their power, we don't normally notice them.

Fan says that the only way a stormquake can hurt you is if you are standing on the ocean floor during a hurricane. "This is the last thing you need to worry about," he adds.

B **Read the article.** Circle **T** for True or **F** for False.

1	Stormquakes last only a few seconds.	T	F
2	Powerful storms create giant waves that cause stormquakes.	T	F
3	The first stormquake happened ten years ago.	T	F
4	Stormquakes endanger many people's lives.	T	F

READING

A Scan the article. What does the discovery tell us about the Earth's climate?

SCIENTISTS DISCOVER MONSTER SNAKE!

A A team of scientists has discovered the bones of a giant snake that lived in the rainforests of Colombia 60 million years ago. They have named it *Titanoboa*, or "the monster snake." It is the largest, longest, and heaviest snake ever discovered.

B Scientists believe Titanoboa was a good swimmer, but they think it was even faster on land. They also think that it ate other giant animals—they found the fossils of giant turtles and crocodiles in the same area. Titanoboa weighed over 1,100 kilograms and was 13 to 15 meters long. It was nearly three times heavier than Gigantophis, the second largest snake ever discovered. This snake lived in North Africa 40 million years ago. It was about 10 meters long and weighed about 450 kilograms.

C Titanoboa belongs to the same family as the anaconda, but it was much larger than its modern cousin. Today's anacondas are around six meters long. The heaviest— South America's green anaconda—weighs about 200 kilograms. This makes Titanoboa more than twice as long as the largest snake alive today, and more than five times heavier.

D The discovery of Titanoboa is important. Its fossil tells us a lot about the history of Earth's climate. Today, large snakes are only found near the equator, where it is hottest. Snakes living farther from the equator are much smaller. Researchers think that Titanoboa could not have grown so big without year-round temperatures of at least 32°C. Because of this, they believe that some places on Earth, like Colombia, were once much warmer.

E Snakes today are much smaller than the giants of long ago. But as climate change continues to warm up the Earth, we have to ask ourselves: will we see the return of giant snakes again in the near future?

B Answer the questions about *Scientists Discover Monster Snake!*

1 DETAIL Why do scientists think Titanoboa ate other large animals?

   a It spent most of its time on land.

   b Gigantophis had a similar diet.

   c They found turtle and crocodile fossils in the area.

2 DETAIL What is true about Titanoboa?

   a It was more than twice as heavy as Gigantophis.

   b It was fast in the water but slow on land.

   c It weighed just under 500 kilograms.

3 PURPOSE What is the purpose of paragraph C?

    a to describe how Titanoboa evolved into the anaconda

    b to compare Titanoboa with today's anaconda

    c to warn about the dangers of encountering an anaconda

4 DETAIL What do scientists think allowed Titanoboa to grow so big?

    a giant prey   **b** more rain   **c** warm temperatures

5 DETAIL The writer suggests that monster snakes could _____ if the Earth gets warmer.

    a go extinct   **b** grow smaller   **c** return

C   EXAM PRACTICE   **Read the article again.** Complete the chart.

Snake	Length	Weight	When it lived	Where it lived
Titanoboa				
Gigantophis				
green anaconda				

VOCABULARY

A   **Complete the sentences.** Circle the correct answers.

1   If an earthquake **destroys** a home, the next step is to *decorate / rebuild* it.

2   If a piece of art is the **original**, it *is / isn't* a copy.

3   You **preserve** something in order to *make it better / keep it as it is*.

4   When we discuss **quality**, we talk about how *good / old* something is.

5   If you **reach** a place, you *leave it / arrive there*.

6   If someone tells you a **secret**, they *want / don't want* you to share it with others.

B   **Match.** Join the people to the things they might study.

1   a paleontologist ○   ○ **a** the effects of social media on our happiness

2   an archaeologist ○   ○ **b** small underwater earthquakes caused by storms

3   a biologist ○   ○ **c** an ancient Maya city deep in the rainforest

4   a psychologist ○   ○ **d** the fossil of a new dinosaur species

5   a geologist ○   ○ **e** what plants would grow well on Mars

WRITING

WRITING TIP **WRITING A NEWS ARTICLE**

News articles are often structured like an upside-down pyramid: the most important information comes first, and the least important information is at the end of the story.

A **Read the news story.** Notice how it is organized.

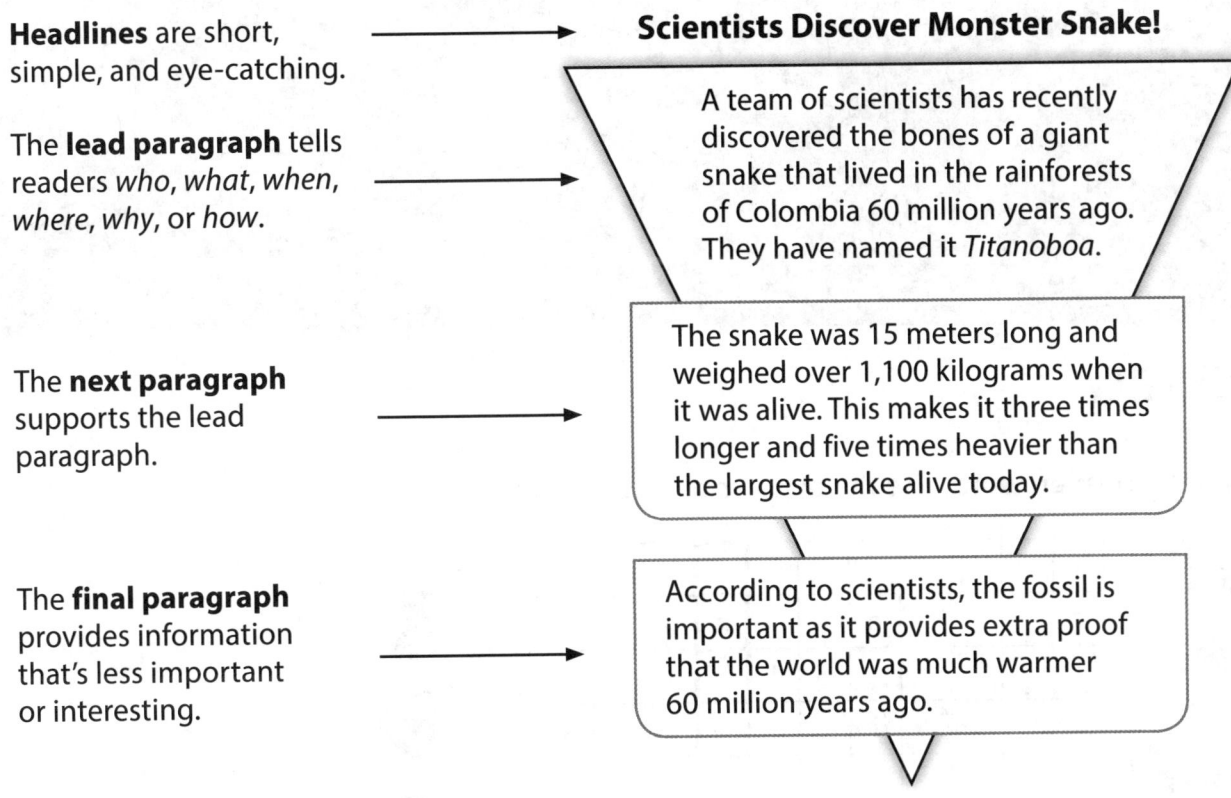

Headlines are short, simple, and eye-catching. → **Scientists Discover Monster Snake!**

The **lead paragraph** tells readers *who*, *what*, *when*, *where*, *why*, or *how*. → A team of scientists has recently discovered the bones of a giant snake that lived in the rainforests of Colombia 60 million years ago. They have named it *Titanoboa*.

The **next paragraph** supports the lead paragraph. → The snake was 15 meters long and weighed over 1,100 kilograms when it was alive. This makes it three times longer and five times heavier than the largest snake alive today.

The **final paragraph** provides information that's less important or interesting. → According to scientists, the fossil is important as it provides extra proof that the world was much warmer 60 million years ago.

B **Imagine something exciting happened at your school.** Make notes. Then organize the details from most important to least important.

C **Write a news story.** Use your notes from **B**. Follow the news story organization in **A**. Then write a headline for your story.

_____

_____

_____

_____

_____

_____

_____

_____

11

BUY ONE, **GET ONE** FREE!

Buy 1 Get 1 FREE
BUY 1 GET 1 FREE
Buy 1 Get 1 FREE
Buy 1 Get 1 FREE
18
ROCKY

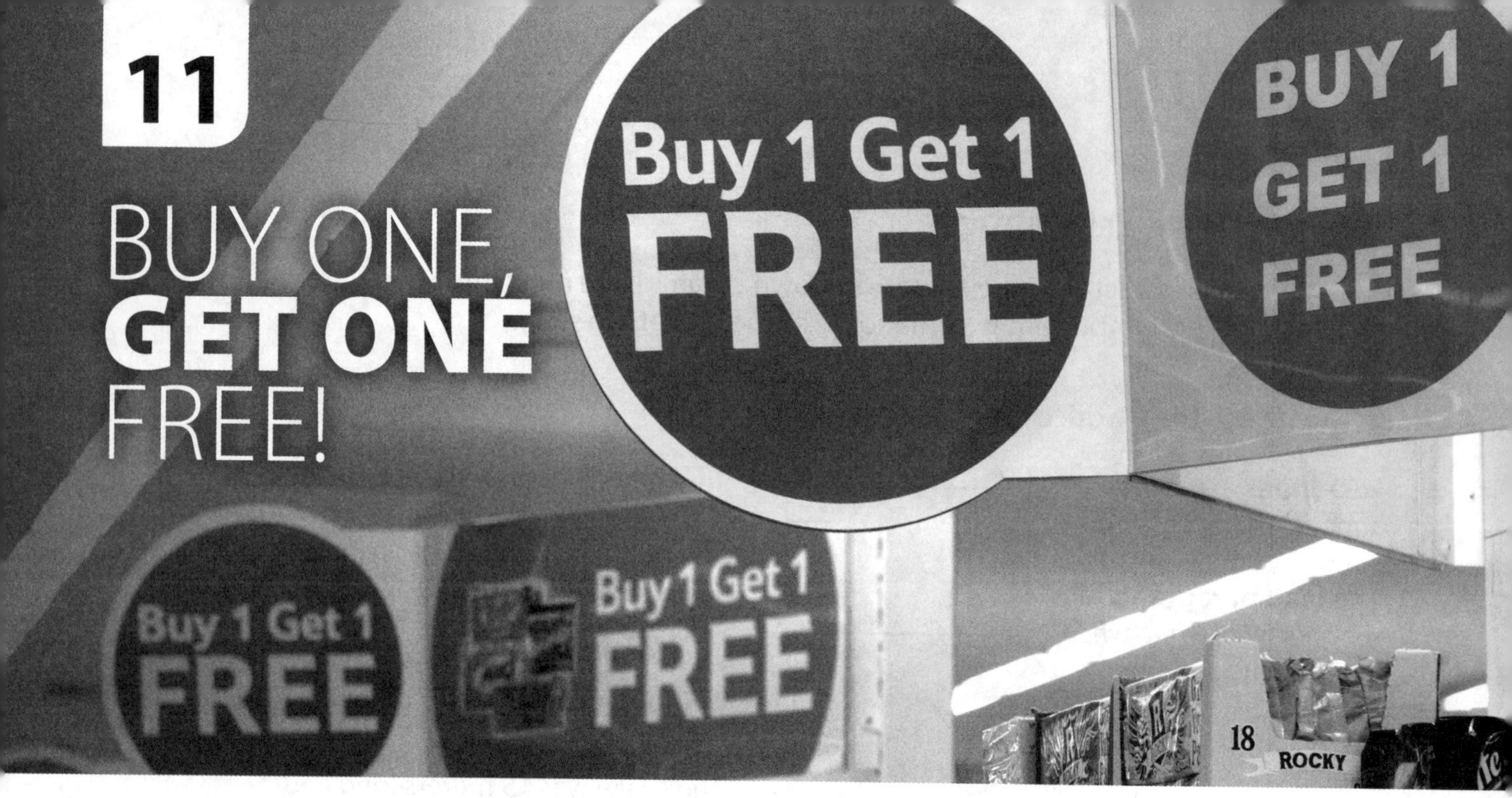

PREVIEW

A **Find the hidden word.** Use the pictures to solve the puzzle.

1 s s
2 o h
3 l l
4 i s
5 t e
6 o o
7 e a

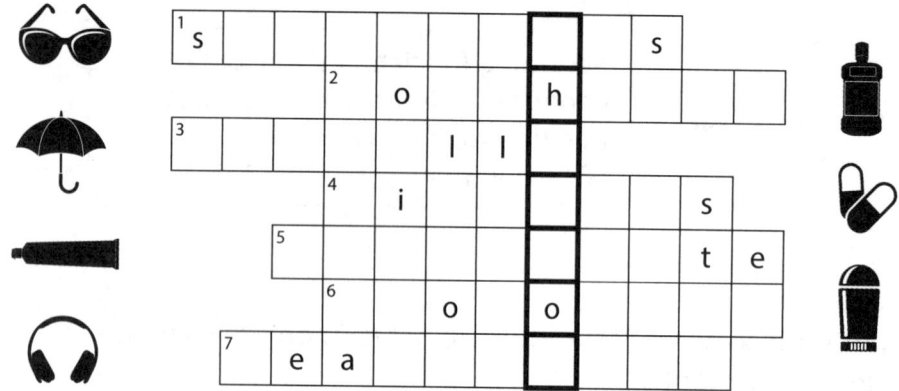

The hidden words is ____________________.

B **Complete the sentences.** Use the words from **A**.

1 Our ____________________ will protect your eyes even on the brightest days.

2 Wear these ____________________ and it will sound like you're at an actual concert!

3 Take these ____________________ each day to stay healthy and strong.

4 Our sports ____________________ will keep you smelling great, even after a long workout.

C **Write.** Which products in **A** do you use? What brands do you use? Why?

____

____

LANGUAGE FOCUS

A **Complete the sentences.** Use the correct form of the verbs in parentheses.

1 If you _____ (**order**) it now, I _____ (**give**) you a discount.

2 If they _____ (**find**) a new fossil, they _____ (**be**) famous.

3 It _____ (**be**) much cheaper if you _____ (**order**) it online.

4 If you _____ (**not accept**) credit cards, I _____ (**pay**) in cash.

5 If you _____ (**not like**) seafood, then I _____ (**not order**) it.

6 _____ they _____ (**do**) if Alan _____ (**not show up**)?

B **Match.** Join the two parts of the sentences together.

1 If this jacket is too small, ◯   ◯ **a** your teeth will be much whiter.

2 If you don't fill in the form, ◯   ◯ **b** I'll go again tomorrow.

3 If you use this discount coupon, ◯   ◯ **c** you can learn more about our product.

4 If the store is closed today, ◯   ◯ **d** you can exchange it for a larger one.

5 If you use this toothpaste, ◯   ◯ **e** you'll get 20 percent off.

6 If you visit our website, ◯   ◯ **f** we can't enter you in the prize draw.

C **Complete the conversation.** Put the words in the correct order.

Alice: Do / want / to / you / the mall / on Saturday / go to

_____?

Mary: If / it'll / we / on the weekend, / go there / be / really crowded

_____.

Alice: But / great deals / of / will be / all kinds / there

_____.

Mary: What / we go / get / kind of / will / we / deals / if

_____?

Alice: Everything / price / at half / will / the usual / be

_____.

Mary: Wow! / should / we / go / definitely

_____!

THE REAL WORLD

PRICING STRATEGIES

A supermarket aisle in Washington State, USA

How much attention do you pay to the price of things at supermarkets? Customers may not realize this, but supermarkets think a lot about how much an item should cost. To find the perfect price, supermarkets use what they call "pricing strategies."

One pricing strategy is called the "loss leader." Some supermarkets sell certain popular items—like milk, bread, and bananas—at very low prices. If shoppers pay very little for these items, they will think that everything else in the store is also cheap. They will then buy other items at regular prices.

Another strategy is "psychological pricing." This strategy makes customers feel like they're spending less than they actually are. Supermarkets often sell items at prices like $2.99 instead of $3.00. Shoppers have a lot on their minds, so they often don't round up these prices. If customers feel like they're spending two dollars for every three dollars they spend, they'll end up buying a lot more things.

A **Read the article.** Circle the correct answers.

1 Supermarkets sell loss leaders at **lower** / **higher** prices than normal.

2 A probable loss-leader item in a supermarket is **eggs** / **fresh shrimp**.

3 Because of psychological pricing, some customers end up paying **more** / **less** than they expected.

4 Shoppers don't round up prices because they are **not good at math** / **busy**.

B **Read the sentences.** Write **L** (loss leader) or **P** (psychological pricing).

_____ "In my head, the total was about $45. But it was actually $55!"

_____ "The eggs were a real bargain. But everything else was expensive."

_____ "I used to get tricked a lot. But these days, I always round up the prices."

_____ "Some of the prices were so low. I thought I was in the cheapest supermarket in town!"

READING

A **Scan the article.** Circle the two companies mentioned.

GUERRILLA MARKETING

Have you ever seen a poster for a product in a place you didn't expect? Or have you ever been surprised by a group of strangers who suddenly started singing and dancing together to promote a service? People in
5 advertising call this "guerrilla marketing." It's a term that describes low-cost and unusual marketing strategies that catch people off guard.

Guerrilla marketing is different from traditional marketing because it doesn't use typical marketing
10 platforms like print, TV, or online advertising. It's also a lot cheaper. It was first designed for small businesses with less money, but these days many large companies are trying this clever and affordable strategy.

A surfer looks for a book at an outdoor IKEA library.

Coca-Cola is one such company. It once placed a special vending machine on a college
15 campus. If students bought a bottle of Coca-Cola from the machine, they got two extra bottles free of charge to give to their friends. Sometimes, a hand came out of the machine and gave customers flowers instead of an extra drink. People loved it! Coca-Cola filmed customers enjoying this special "happiness machine" and posted the video online. Many people watched the video and shared it with their friends, and the company enjoyed
20 free publicity.

IKEA—one of the world's largest furniture companies—also gave guerrilla marketing a try. To celebrate the 30th anniversary of its most popular bookcase, IKEA decided to try something different. It teamed up with a charity called the Australian Literacy and Numeracy Foundation to set up the world's largest outdoor library. The location? On a
25 beach! IKEA displayed its bookcases on Sydney's Bondi Beach and filled them with over 6,000 books. People got to see IKEA's bookcase in use and find something interesting to read at the same time.

B **Answer the questions about *Guerrilla Marketing*.**

1 PURPOSE What is the purpose of the first paragraph?

   a to describe the origins of guerrilla marketing

   b to show why guerrilla marketing is effective

   c to explain what guerrilla marketing is

2 VOCABULARY What does *off guard* (line 7) mean?

   a at a bad time   **b** doing something unusual   **c** not expecting a surprise

3 DETAIL Coca-Cola got free publicity because students _____ the "happiness machine" video.

   a made   **b** shared   **c** paid for

4 INFERENCE IKEA probably chose Bondi Beach to show its products because _____.

   a it was an unusual place to see books

   b it was near to a public library

   c it was the future location of one of its stores

5 INFERENCE IKEA not only advertised their bookcase, but also _____.

   a sold books   **b** supported a charity   **c** exchanged furniture

B EXAM PRACTICE **What does the reading say about guerrilla marketing?** Check (✓) the correct sentences.

☐ It catches people by surprise.

☐ It is often cheaper than traditional marketing.

☐ It is more effective than traditional marketing.

☐ It works better on young people.

☐ It can be used by small and large companies.

VOCABULARY

A **Complete the sentences.** Use the words in the box.

> afford   benefit   donate   care   publicity   values

1 She tries to _____ money to her favorite charity every month.

2 I can't _____ this phone right now. I'll wait until it goes on sale.

3 They hope that many children will _____ from the new hospital.

4 Our organization got free _____ when it appeared on the evening news.

5 The company doesn't _____ about the damage it's doing to the river.

6 I like this company because it shares my _____ about the environment.

B **Complete the sentences.** Circle the correct answers.

1 **Advertising** / **Profit** is a great way to get your product noticed by many people.

2 They increased their **publicity** / **profits** by switching to cheaper materials.

3 We increased **sales** / **marketing** by opening shops in other countries.

4 People all over the world recognize our company's **sales** / **brand**.

5 Their **marketing** / **brand** team came up with a clever idea for an ad campaign.

WRITING

WRITING TIP   **WRITING AN AD**

How do ads persuade people to buy products? They show how their product is different from other products and why buying it is a good idea. This is best done with simple and descriptive language.

A   Read the model ad. Notice how it is organized.

Open with a catchy slogan. ———————►	Whatever the time zone, we've got you covered!
Use descriptive language. ———————►	Time Zones travel shampoo will keep your hair looking soft, smooth, and shiny anywhere in the world!
Explain why your product is special. ——►	Our all-natural shampoo will keep your hair clean and healthy in any weather. And with our long-lasting formula, your hair will smell great even after a 15-hour flight!
Include an offer. ———————————►	Don't let a bad hair day ruin your adventure. If you buy one bottle of Time Zones today, you'll get another one free.
Close with your slogan. ——————————►	Time Zones. We've got you covered!

B   Choose a product. Think of a catchy slogan and reasons why your product is special. Make notes.

C   Write an ad. Use your notes from **B**. Use descriptive language, and include your slogan and an offer.

_____

_____

_____

_____

_____

_____

_____

_____

12

WHICH PLANET IS **THE BIGGEST?**

PREVIEW

A Complete the sentences. Use the words in the box.

> Earth   moon   planet   solar system

1 The sun is the star at the center of our _____ .

2 Mercury is the closest _____ to our sun.

3 The _____ is the brightest object in our night sky.

4 _____ is between Venus and Mars.

B Rank the following from biggest (1) to smallest (5).

_____ Earth   _____ the sun   _____ the moon   _____ our solar system   __1__ our galaxy

C Research. Write the planets of our solar system in order of size. Then write a sentence to help you remember the order.

biggest ←————————————————————————————→ smallest

			Neptune	Earth			

_____

LANGUAGE FOCUS

A Read the questions. Then answer them using complete sentences and the words in parentheses.

1 What will Lily be doing at noon? (**have lunch**)
   She'll be having lunch.

2 Where will she be going after that? (**the library**)
   _____

3 What will she be doing there? (**working on a project**)
   _____

4 Will she be working on her project alone? (**no**).
   _____

5 Who will she be working with? (**Justina**)
   _____

6 When will she be presenting her project? (**Friday**)
   _____

B Complete the paragraph. Circle the correct answers.

[1] **Have tourists visited / Will tourists visit** space in the future? One private company thinks so. If things go well, the Gateway Foundation [2] **is sending /will be sending** regular people to space very soon. It [3] **developed / has developed** plans to build what it calls the first "spaceport"—a giant hotel in space for tourists to stay at. The spaceport [4] **has orbited / will orbit** Earth, and [5] **has allowed / will allow** many scientists and tourists to live in space for long periods of time. If the company's plan [6] **is / will be** successful, trips to space [7] **will last / are lasting** a lot longer than they do now.

C Complete the conversation. Number the sentences in the correct order.

a _____ Yes. I've looked everywhere, but I can't find them. I guess I'll have to start over.

b _____ You will? Thanks, Rachel. That's really nice of you.

c _____ I thought I was, but my computer crashed and I've lost my slides.

d __1__ Hi, Chris. What are you doing?

e _____ That sounds interesting. Are you almost done?

f _____ Oh, no! Have you checked your hard drive? Maybe you saved them there.

g _____ Well, don't worry, Chris. If you want, I'll help you.

h _____ Oh, hi Rachel. I'm working on my Jupiter presentation. I'll be presenting it in class tomorrow.

THE REAL WORLD

A NASA astronaut at work outside the International Space Station

A **Skim the article.** Choose the best title.

a Heroes of Apollo 13   b Space Emergencies   c How to Fix a Rocket

Being an astronaut seems like a fun and exciting job, but it's also full of danger. Since the first human flew to space in 1957, there have been many space emergencies.

Perhaps the most famous space emergency happened during the Apollo 13 mission in 1970. The spacecraft was on its way to the moon when an oxygen tank exploded. The astronauts on board had to figure out how to get back home quickly before they ran out of air. But first, they needed a way to repair the spacecraft's CO_2 system to keep the air they had left breathable. They figured out a solution—using just a sock and some tape!

Fire is also a big danger in space. It can destroy equipment and burn through oxygen supplies, and there's nowhere to escape to. In 1997, a fire broke out on the Russian MIR space station. It burned for almost 15 minutes, filling the space station with smoke. "The fire was so hot that it was melting metal," remembers American astronaut Jerry Linenger. Luckily, he and the other astronauts were able to put out the fire before it got too big.

B **Read the article.** Circle the correct answers.

1 The Apollo 13 astronauts **landed / didn't land** on the moon.

2 There was **a fire / an explosion** aboard the Apollo 13 spacecraft.

3 According to the article, fires in space are more dangerous than fires on Earth because **they burn hotter / there's nowhere to escape to**.

4 Jerry Linenger **helped put out / died in** the MIR space station fire.

READING

A **Skim the text.** Underline the names of the spacecraft, landers, and rovers that went to Mars.

THE SEARCH FOR LIFE ON MARS

Are we alone in the universe? People have always wondered about life on other planets. And for many years, scientists at NASA have been searching one planet in particular for signs of life: Mars.

5 In 1975, NASA put two landers—Viking 1 and 2—on the red planet's surface. The landers sent many pictures of the planet's surface back to Earth. Many years later, NASA sent another spacecraft. The Mars Odyssey entered Mars's orbit in 2001. Its mission was to look for water. The spacecraft
10 orbited the planet and sent back photos that showed ice buried under the surface. They also showed that Mars once had lakes and rivers. This excited scientists. If water once flowed on Mars, maybe there was once life there, too.

The Viking 1 lander took this photo of Mars's surface on July 20, 1976.

NASA's next step was to send rovers—a type of wheeled robot—to Mars. In 2004, Spirit
15 and Opportunity landed on Mars. They found not just water, but signs of volcanic activity. This suggested that Mars was once a lot like Earth. In 2011, NASA sent another rover named Curiosity. This rover had much better instruments, such as lasers and an X-ray machine. Its mission was to look for signs of life and to find out if Mars once had the conditions needed to support life. Curiosity is still on Mars trying to complete its mission. Since landing, it has
20 sent a lot of useful information back to Earth.

In the future, NASA will be sending more rovers to Mars. These will have even better instruments than the rovers before them. NASA hopes that the information these rovers send back will help answer the question once and for all: "Was there ever life on Mars?"

B **Answer the questions about *The Search for Life on Mars*.**

1 DETAIL The main mission of NASA's Mars Odyssey was to _____ .

   a take photographs of Mars's surface

   b look for water on Mars

   c look for signs of life on Mars

2 DETAIL Which of these did not land on Mars?

   a Viking 1 b Odyssey c Curiosity

3 INFERENCE What could Spirit and Opportunity do that Viking 1 and 2 couldn't?

   a land on Mars's surface

   b move around on Mars's surface

   c take photographs of Mars's surface

4 VOCABULARY In the final sentence, *once and for all* means _____ .

    a finally   **b** especially   **c** easily

5 MAIN IDEA What's the best answer to the question, "Was there ever life on Mars?"

    a Definitely not.   **b** Maybe.   **c** Definitely.

C EXAM PRACTICE **Read the sentences.** Circle **T** for True, **F** for False, or **NG** for Not Given.

  1 Both Viking 1 and Viking 2 landed on Mars in 1975.   **T**   **F**   **NG**

  2 Odyssey found lakes and rivers full of water on Mars.   **T**   **F**   **NG**

  3 Spirit and Opportunity found many volcanoes on Mars.   **T**   **F**   **NG**

  4 Curiosity used its lasers to collect rock samples.   **T**   **F**   **NG**

  5 NASA will be sending bigger rovers to Mars in the future.   **T**   **F**   **NG**

VOCABULARY

A **Complete the sentences.** Circle the correct answers.

  1 If something lasts **forever**, it *ends immediately / never ends*.

  2 If you **locate** something, you discover *what caused it / where it is*.

  3 An **object** is a thing you can *only imagine / see and touch*.

  4 If an object **reflects** light, *light passes through it / it sends light back*.

  5 When someone improves **significantly**, they improve *a little / a lot*.

  6 The **surface** of a lake is the *top / bottom* part.

B **Complete the sentences.** Use the words in the box with the suffix *-like*.

> business   child   dream   Earth   life   star

  1 People were amazed by the movie Jurassic Park because the dinosaurs were so _____ .

  2 That small _____ object that's moving across the sky quickly is actually a satellite.

  3 Her mother sounds very young—she has a very _____ voice.

  4 Auroras are amazing. There's something unreal and almost _____ about them.

  5 I don't find him friendly—he talks to us in a way that's very _____ .

  6 I hope we someday find a planet with _____ conditions.

WRITING

WRITING TIP **WRITING AN OPINION PARAGRAPH**

When writing an opinion paragraph, you need to organize your ideas well. It also helps to use expressions like *think*, *believe*, *feel*, and *in my opinion*.

A Read the paragraph. Underline the verbs and phrases that express opinions.

State both sides of an issue. ⟶ Space travel is exciting and educational. But some think it's too expensive.

State your opinion. ⟶ Personally, I believe that we should continue exploring space. Here's why.

First, we learn many things from space travel. These things are very useful here on Earth. Second, our planet is crowded. We need to find a second home for humans before we run out of space.

Give reasons for your opinion. ⟶

Acknowledge but argue against the main counterarguments. ⟶ It is true that there are other big problems on Earth that we need to fix. But I feel it's possible to fix these problems and explore space at the same time.

Summarize your opinion and the main reason. ⟶ In my opinion, space travel is important. I believe that the things we learn from it will help us fix Earth's problems.

B Answer one of the questions below. State your opinion and list reasons, but consider both sides of the issue. Make notes.

Should humans colonize Mars?
Do teachers give too much homework?

Does technology help students learn?
Should video gaming be considered a sport?

C Write an opinion paragraph. Use your notes from **B**. Include opinion verbs and phrases.

_____

_____

_____

_____

_____

_____

_____

_____

LANGUAGE NOTES

UNIT 1 I'D LIKE TO BE A PILOT

TALKING ABOUT CAREER GOALS (USING *WANT* AND *WOULD LIKE*)	
What kind of job **do** you **want**? What kind of job **would** you **like**?	I **want** a job **that** pays a lot of money. I**'d like** a job **that allows** me **to** travel. I**'d like** a job **that involves** working with animals.
What **do** you **want to be** someday? What **would** you **like to do** someday?	I **want to be** a vet. I**'d like to be** a flight attendant. I**'d love to** work as an app developer.

UNIT 2 WHICH ONE IS BRUNO?

IDENTIFYING AND DESCRIBING PEOPLE (USING *THE ONE WHO* AND ADJECTIVES)		
Identifying people	**Which one** is Tyler?	He's **the one who** called yesterday. He's **the one (who's)** watching TV.
	Which ones are your cousins?	They're **the ones** by the door / in green T-shirts.
Describing personality	**What's** Miguel **like**?	He's a little shy / kind of quiet.
	What are your cousins **like**?	They're really outgoing / a lot of fun.

UNIT 3 WE HAVE TO REDUCE TRASH!

TALKING ABOUT RULES (USING *HAVE TO, ALLOWED TO,* AND *CAN*)	
You **have to** bring your own bags to this store. He isn't **allowed to** put that in this bin. She **can** leave her plastic waste here.	
Do I **have to** bring my own bag?	Yes, you **do**. / No, you **don't**.
Can I leave my trash here?	Yes, you **can**. / No, you **can't**.
Am I **allowed to** throw my trash here?	Yes, you **are**. / No, you**'re not**. / No, you **aren't**.

UNIT 4 HOW DO SLOTHS MOVE?

DESCRIBING CHARACTERISTICS AND BEHAVIOR (USING ADJECTIVES AND ADVERBS)

		Adjectives	Adverbs
Sloths are **slow** and **quiet**. Dolphins are **good** swimmers. Bees are **hard** workers.	Sloths move **slowly** and **quietly**. Dolphins swim **well**. Bees work **hard**.	slow easy bad	slow**ly** eas**ily** bad**ly**
How does an owl wait?	It waits **patiently**.	good fast hard	**well** **fast** **hard**

UNIT 5 I'M MEETING FRIENDS LATER

TALKING ABOUT FUTURE EVENTS AND PLANS (USING SIMPLE PRESENT AND PRESENT PROGRESSIVE)

Scheduled future events	Future plans
I **have** a class in the morning. The train **arrives** at 9:30. What time **does** the party **start**? It **starts** at 7:00.	I**'m meeting** friends on Saturday. He**'s watching** a soccer match this weekend. What **are** you **doing** in the evening? I**'m going** to the park.

UNIT 6 WHAT WILL EARTH BE LIKE IN THE FUTURE?

MAKING PREDICTIONS (USING *WILL, WON'T, MORE, FEWER*, AND *LESS*)

What **will** the future **be like**?	It**'ll be** hotter and drier. There**'ll be more** wildfires. There**'ll be more** pollution. There**'ll be fewer** animals. There**'ll be less** food.
Will there **be** a lot more people?	Yes, there **will**. There**'ll** (definitely) **be** a lot more people. No, there **won't**. There (probably) **won't be** a lot more people.
Do you think food prices **will increase**?	Yes, I do. I think they**'ll increase**. No, I don't. I don't think they**'ll increase**.

UNIT 7 WHEN DID IT HAPPEN?

TALKING ABOUT PAST EVENTS (USING *WHEN*, *HOW LONG*, AND PREPOSITIONS OF TIME)	
A point in time	
When was the first soccer World Cup final?	It was **in** 1930. / It was **on** July 30, 1930.
How long ago were the first Olympic Games?	They were over 2,700 years **ago**.
A period of time	
When did Cleopatra live?	She lived **from** 69 B.C. **to** 30 B.C.
How long was Marco Polo in China?	He was there **for** 17 years.

UNIT 8 HAVE YOU EVER TRIED GO-KARTING?

TALKING ABOUT PAST EXPERIENCES (USING PRESENT PERFECT)	
Have you **ever had** Moroccan food?	Yes, I **have**. I**'ve had** it several times.
	No, I **haven't**. I**'ve never** tried it.
Has she **tried** indoor rock climbing?	Yes, she **has**. She went last year.
	No, she **hasn't**. She**'s** never **done** it.
I**'ve been** to the zoo a couple of times.	Me too. / I **have**, too.
	Oh, really? I **haven't**.
He**'s never gone** surfing.	Me neither. / Neither **have** I.
	Oh, really? I **have**.

UNIT 9 PHONES USED TO BE MUCH BIGGER!

DESCRIBING PAST STATES AND ACTIVITIES (USING *USED TO*)	
States	Phones **used to be** much bigger in the past.
	This phone didn't **use to cost** so much.
Activities	My mother **used to write** me letters, but now she emails.
	When I was young, I **never used to shop** online. Now I do it all the time.
Questions	**Did** she **use to** send you emails?
	Did your grandfather **use to** call you every day?

UNIT 10 THEY'VE MADE AN AMAZING DISCOVERY!

DESCRIBING PAST ACTIONS (USING SIMPLE PAST AND PRESENT PERFECT)

Simple past	Present perfect
I **applied** for membership last week.	I**'ve** (just) **gotten** my membership card.
They **arrived at the hotel** three hours ago.	They**'ve** (just) **gone** to the museum.
Where **did** she **go**? She **went** to the lab.	Where **has** she **gone**? She**'s gone** to the lab.
Duration of continuing actions	
How long have you been a member?	I**'ve been** a member **for** a year.
	I**'ve been** a member **since** last year.

UNIT 11 BUY ONE, GET ONE FREE!

TALKING ABOUT RESULTS (USING FIRST CONDITIONALS)

If you **buy** a bottle, you**'ll get** another one free.	
If you **download** our app, you **can ask** for a free sample.	
Your hair **will be** much shinier **if** you **use** this shampoo for a week.	
If you **use** it daily, you **won't have to worry** about bad breath.	
If you **aren't** happy, the store **will give** you your money back.	
If you **don't buy** it today, you **won't be able to buy** it later.	
If I buy three, **will** I get a discount?	Yes, you **will**. / No, you **won't**.
What **will** you **do if** the store **is** closed?	I**'ll** go to another store.

UNIT 12 WHICH PLANET IS THE BIGGEST?

USING DIFFERENT TENSES

Describing future activities	Future progressive	At 5 p.m. tomorrow, I**'ll be doing** my homework.
		This time next week, I**'ll be giving** a presentation.
Tense review	Present progressive	I**'m doing** some research at the moment.
	Present perfect	I**'ve** (just) **finished** working on my space project.
	Future with *will*	People **will** (probably) **live** on Mars someday.
	First conditional	**If** I do well, I**'ll win** a trip to space camp!

CREDITS

Photo Credits

Text Credits